THE STORM BOAT KINGS

To my maternal grandfather, Corporal Hugh Barton,
who gave up six years of his life to serve in the
Royal Canadian Engineers

THE STORM BOAT

KINGS

23rd Field Company
Royal Canadian
Engineers at
Arnhem
1944

John Sliz

Travelogue 219 Publishing
Durham, Canada

TL219-329 MGES-11 `Storm Boat Kings' Second Edition, July 2023
Published by: Travelogue 219
          Durham, Canada
ISBN 978-1-990653-12-4

Unless otherwise noted, all charts and drawings by John Sliz.

Front cover main photo: part of John Cronyn's 1st Platoon at the opening of Monty Bridge. Major Tucker is on the far left with Lt. Cronyn to his left. Sergenat Willick is to his left with Corporal Ryan directly behind him. On the far right is David Hope. Junior Goodall snuck in for the shot to stand to his right. Magnusson is with the shovel. (Luuk Buist)

Top right: Russ Kennedy is at the controls of a Storm Boat. (Russ Kennedy)

All other photos can be found in the book.

Table of Contents

Preface and Acknowledgments

*"The night was made for clandestine exits. It was
very dark with an inky sky and there was a
strong wind and persistent heavy rain."* [1]

Major-General Urquhart CB, DSO

By the time the Royal Canadian Engineers (RCE) were
involved in Operation Market Garden, the great gamble that was
supposed to end the war by Christmas had already failed. Simply
put, the fact that they were in action meant that something had
not gone according to plan, signifying that at least one of the
bridges along the British 2nd Army's attack route had not been
taken and that their Storm boats were required to move troops
across a river, one way or another.

Bridging rivers was one of the special tasks that the members
of the 1st Canadian Army Troops, Royal Canadian Engineers
(ICAT, RCE) had done since they arrived in Normandy during
the summer of 1944. They were specially trained in crossing
broad and tricky waters and this was why they had been rushed
200 miles to Bourg-Leopold, Belgium on September 16th - one day
before the operation was to commence. They were to be part of a
special bridging force made up of 9000 sappers, both British and
Canadian, and 2277 vehicles.

This force was assembled as an `insurance plan' in case one of
the many bridges along the narrow attack corridor had not been
captured. Each unit of this force had been assigned a sector and,
according to the plan, the fact that the 1st Canadian Army
Troops, RCE were required meant that the Neder Rijn (lower
Rhine River sometimes referred to as the `Lek') had to be
crossed.

However, when the 23rd Field Company, RCE was finally called upon to cross the Neder Rijn, it was not to snatch victory from the enemy's grasp, but to minimize Operation Market Garden's failure by evacuating as many of the besieged Airborne troops as possible. In this task, codenamed Operation Berlin, the 23rd succeeded admirably. Under atrocious conditions they ferried the majority of the 2406 (exact figures differ - some say 2396, others higher) men across to safety; including 1794 members of the British 1st Airborne Division; 450 Glider pilots; 42 men of the 1st Independent Polish Parachute Brigade; and 75 men of the Dorsetshire Regiment. It has also been reported that at least one Dutch civilian and one German POW insisted on not being left behind.

If these troops hadn't been evacuated, one wonders how many of the besieged troops would have chosen to die fighting rather than surrender; or, would have died needlessly as the increasing pressure from the German forces tore apart their weakening defenses one group at a time. Nine days of intense fighting had certainly taken its toll on the men trapped inside the Oosterbeek perimeter. Due to the loss of their original drop zones, and a breakdown of communication with the RAF to designate new zones to drop supplies, the division found itself dangerously short of ammunition, food and medical supplies. The British 1st Airborne Division was in grave danger of becoming extinct.

In war many good men die, but thanks to the selfless actions of the RCE and RE (Royal Engineers) many good men lived to fight another day. Their story is told from the viewpoint of these sappers - in particular, from that of the 23rd Field Company, RCE. This was the unit that ferried the majority of the men across the river.

To quote the *Maple Leaf Paper*, the Canadian Army Overseas newspaper: *"The 23rd Field Company, Royal Canadian Engineers, merited world acclaim for their grim job of evacuating 2,400 airborne men from the tip of the Arnhem salient weeks ago when they crossed the Lek under murderous enemy fire..."* [2] This story was repeated by news media outlets throughout Canada and the men of the unit were celebrated in local newspapers with bylines such as `Carmichael Man Hero Of Arnhem'. Even the BBC was praising them, much to the annoyance of the British Sappers who were also at Arnhem. To quote the 260th Field Company, RE War Diary: "Worse thing when radio announced 2 days later that the job was done by Canadians." 3 For awhile, the 23rd Field Company, RCE were in the spotlight, but to this day, many of the men who were evacuated by them still didn't know who they were. Even if they did find out who had saved them, only the same rehashed pieces of the story were available to them. Unfortunately, several errors have been reprinted in various accounts and are now accepted as truth. For example: Lieutenant Russ Kennedy has been credited with taking over a boatload of lifebelts on his final crossing, to distribute to the troops he could not take on his Storm boat, while in fact he never saw a lifebelt during the entire operation.4

One of things that puzzled me is where did the two Canadian engineering companies come from? The closest that a unit of the Canadian 1st Army - of which the engineers were a part - was on the opposite side of Brussels working their way up the coast of Belgium. So their presence had to be planned. I looked through my collection of books on the Battle of Arnhem and found that their story is barely mentioned. The engineers who participated in Operation Berlin (the codename of the evacuation) rarely receive more than a paragraph or two, despite the fact there were 4 engineering companies working that night. I already have in my collection dozens of books telling the story of the Airborne troops, but not one for the engineers. Why not? To my knowledge, none existed.

So I knew that I had to do some research. Fortunately, I got help from several sources. Philip Reinders and Peter Vrolijk of the Arnhem Battle Research Group in Holland, sent me everything they had on these mysterious Canadians. This included not only war diaries and maps, but all of their research on Operation Berlin, as well. They asked me if I wouldn't mind taking over the project. A friend of theirs, Luuk Buist sent me all the material he had as well. This was the first time that I had heard of `The Twenty-Third Story'. This book was put out by Major Mike

Tucker, the OC of the 23rd Field Company, RCE shortly after the war ended. My research was now well underway and with the help of the internet, I made contact with Colonel Ken Holmes of the Canadian Military Engineer museum near Fredericton, NB. He provided me with the names and addresses of the remaining members of the old unit. I wrote to them all. In addition, Ken Holmes obtained some hard to get files from the archives in Ottawa and, as the author of *The History of the Corps of Royal Canadian Engineers Volume III,* has allowed me to benefit from his experience.

Lieutenant Russ Kennedy first agreed to answer a few of my questions, and has since provided me with pages of answers and memories. And if that wasn't enough, he gave me a copy of his privately published memoir, *Whispers and Shadows.*

From Sergeant George King and his wife Ethel I received a dozen or so unpublished photos and old newspaper clippings on the 23rd Field Company, RCE.

I also wish to thank John Cronyn, Clayton Moss, Willie Richardson and Stan Goodall, who all took the time to tell me their version of the events leading up to and including that rainy night in September 1944. They were all too polite to complain, but I'm pretty sure that I disturbed more than a few unpleasant memories.

Even though I had a lot of information, there were some questions that I still needed answered. The only way to answer them was to walk the battlefield so I could see things for myself. It is my belief that the only way to fully understand a battle is to see the lay of the land and to imagine the situation at the time.

On one very hot day during 2003, Philip, Peter, my wife and I crossed the Driel ferry and walked along the winter dyke towards the 23rd embarkation site. With permission from the local residents we wandered along the south bank, looking for clues from the events that happened many years ago. Unfortunately, the river and its banks have changed so much over the years that it was impossible to tell the exact location of the launching and refueling beaches. Since the evacuation happened during a particularly wet period, those beaches might have changed the next week, if not the following day. The culvert where the aid station was located had been filled in, but was still there. A very defensive sheep that never stopped challenging us the entire time we were wandering around now guards it. Another culvert just west of this one remains unchanged so I was able to see what the aid station would have looked like during the operation. After careful study I am sure that we know the exact route that the 23rd took that night to get down to the river.

I would like to thank Adrian Groenweg of the Airborne Museum in Oosterbeek, Holland for allowing me to go through their records and also for taking me on a tour of the area. Also, special thanks to Captain Chad Rizzato of the CME Gagetown and RSM Kevin Patterson of CFB Petawawa for searching through their base's records and sending me what they had.

I wish to thank everyone else whose knowledge and expertise added to this project. They felt that the story about what the 23rd Field Company, RCE did that night was long overdue. When I spoke to the few remaining members of the 23rd, all of them were pleased that someone was interested in doing their story. However, I think that Sgt. George King's wife, Ethel, summed it up best when she said, *"It is about time that someone is doing their story. You know they have <u>really</u> been overshadowed."* [5]

Now, many decades later, here is the long forgotten and hardly ever told story of a small group of Canadians who were sent into The Netherlands with American and British equipment to rescue British and Polish troops while under heavy fire from the Germans.

John Sliz

Glossary

ICAT	1st Canadian Army Troops	Cpl.	Corporal
IICAT	2nd Canadian Army Troops	CQMS	Company Quartermaster Sergeant
AA	Anti-Aircraft		
Abn	Airborne	CRE	Commander Royal Engineers
ADS	Advanced Dressing Station	CSM	Company Sergeant Major
AGRE	Army Group Royal Engineers – consists of 2 or more CAT,RCE.	Det	Detachment; a subunit no longer operating with its parent unit
Bn.	Battalion	Div.	Division
BR or Br	Bridge or bridging. It could also be used for British.	DUKW	A large amphibious truck
		E+M	Electrical and mechanical platoon
CAT	Canadian Army Troops, Royal Canadian Engineers – usually made up of 3 field companies and a field park company.	Engrs	Engineers
		Eqpt.	Equipment
		FBE	Folding Bridge Equipment
		FC	Field Company
CCP	Company Command Post	Fd.	Field
Class 9	A designation for a bridge or raft that can take loads up to and including 9 tons. ie, most medium trucks and jeeps.	Fd. Pk.	Field Park
		Grillage	Protective flooring for bridges
		Groyn	A Dutch term for rock berms extending into rivers to control the current and help reduce the deposit of silt
Class 40	A designation for a bridge or raft that can take loads up to and including 40 tons.		
		GT	General Transport
CME	Canadian Military Engineers	HP	Horsepower
CO	Commanding officer	HQ	Headquarters
Coln	Column	Hrs	Hours
COTC	Canadian Officer Training Corps	i/c	In Command
		KOSB	King's Own Scottish Borders regiment, part of
Coy.	Company		

	the 1st Airborne Division	RSM	Regimental Sergeant Major
LAD	Light Aid Detachment. RCEME assigned to a unit to keep their vehicles running.	RV	Rendezvous
L/Sgt.	Lance Sergeant	Sapper	In the Engineer Corps is the equivalent to a Private in the Infantry or a Gunner in the Artillery. He is the lowest rank in the Engineer Corps and the name Sapper can be traced back to a time when trenches or `saps' were needed for advancing troops to use as cover when they were approaching an enemy fortress. The men who specialized in digging these protective holes or `saps' were called Sappers.
Lt	Lieutenant		
Lt-Col	Lieutenant-Colonel		
MG	Machine gun		
M/Tug	A motorized tug boat used in the building of pontoon and bailey bridges.		
MP	Military police		
NCO	Non-commissioned officer		
Neder Rijn	The Dutch name for the Lower Rhine River, also called, `Lek'.		
		SBF	Special Bridging Force
OC	Officer Commanding	Sgt.	Sergeant
Offrs	Officers	Somerfeld	Metal ramps for bridges
`O' Group	Orders group; a meeting of command personnel used to allocate specific orders to subunits.	SORE	Staff Officer, Royal Engineers
		Spr	Sapper
Op	Operation	Stonk	An artillery barrage
QM	Quartermaster	The Island	The area of land in eastern Holland; between north to south, the Lower Rhine river and the Waal river; and east to west, the Rhine river and the boggy area where the Waal and Lower Rhine nearly meet.
RAP	Regimental aid post		
RASC	Royal Army Service Corps		
RCASC	Royal Canadian Army Service Corps		
RCCS	Royal Canadian Corps of Signals		
RCE	Royal Canadian Engineers	Tippers	Dump trucks
		Tps	Troops
RCEME	Royal Canadian Electrical and Mechanical Engineers	Vehs	Vehicles
		XXX Corps	British 30 Corps
RE	Royal Engineers		
Recce	Reconnaissance		

Above: Lieutenant Russ Kennedy. Originally No. 2 Platoon's commander, but when Bob Tate transferred into the company from 10th Field Park Company, RCE he became the new commander while Russ became the reconnaissance officer. (Russ Kennedy)

A Brief History of the 23rd Field Company, R.C.E.

The 23rd Field Company, RCE was formed on 25 April 1942 in Halifax and Saint John with volunteers from the provinces of Nova Scotia and New Brunswick, including a substantial contingent of coal miners from Glace Bay. The officers came mostly from Ontario and in early 1943 they were joined by two young lieutenants; James Russell Martin and Russell Jordan Kennedy. Martin and Kennedy had both graduated from the Engineering Department at Queen's University in Kingston, Ontario, but they didn't meet until October 1st, 1941 when they were in a recruiting office in Toronto. Since they both had engineering degrees and two years of COTC training at Queen's they were both immediately qualified as second lieutenants and posted to the Eastern Ontario Officer Training Centre at Brockville. After graduation they were posted to Petawawa where they learned how to control men for engineering tasks. They must have done really well because, much to their disappointment, they both

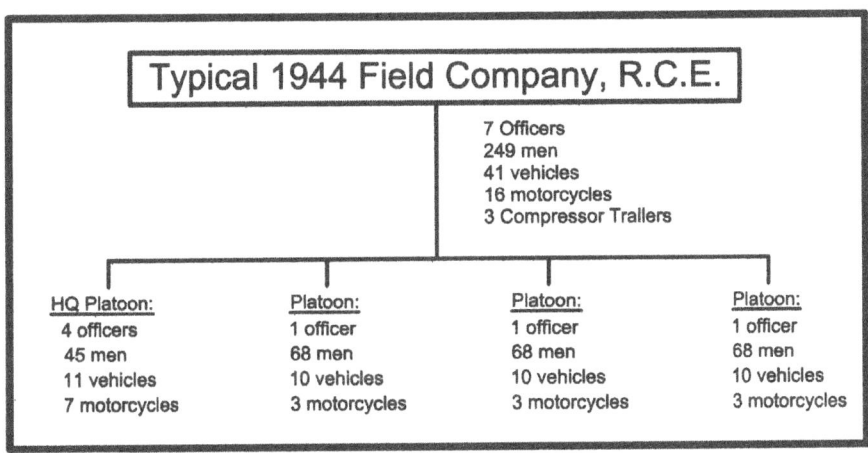

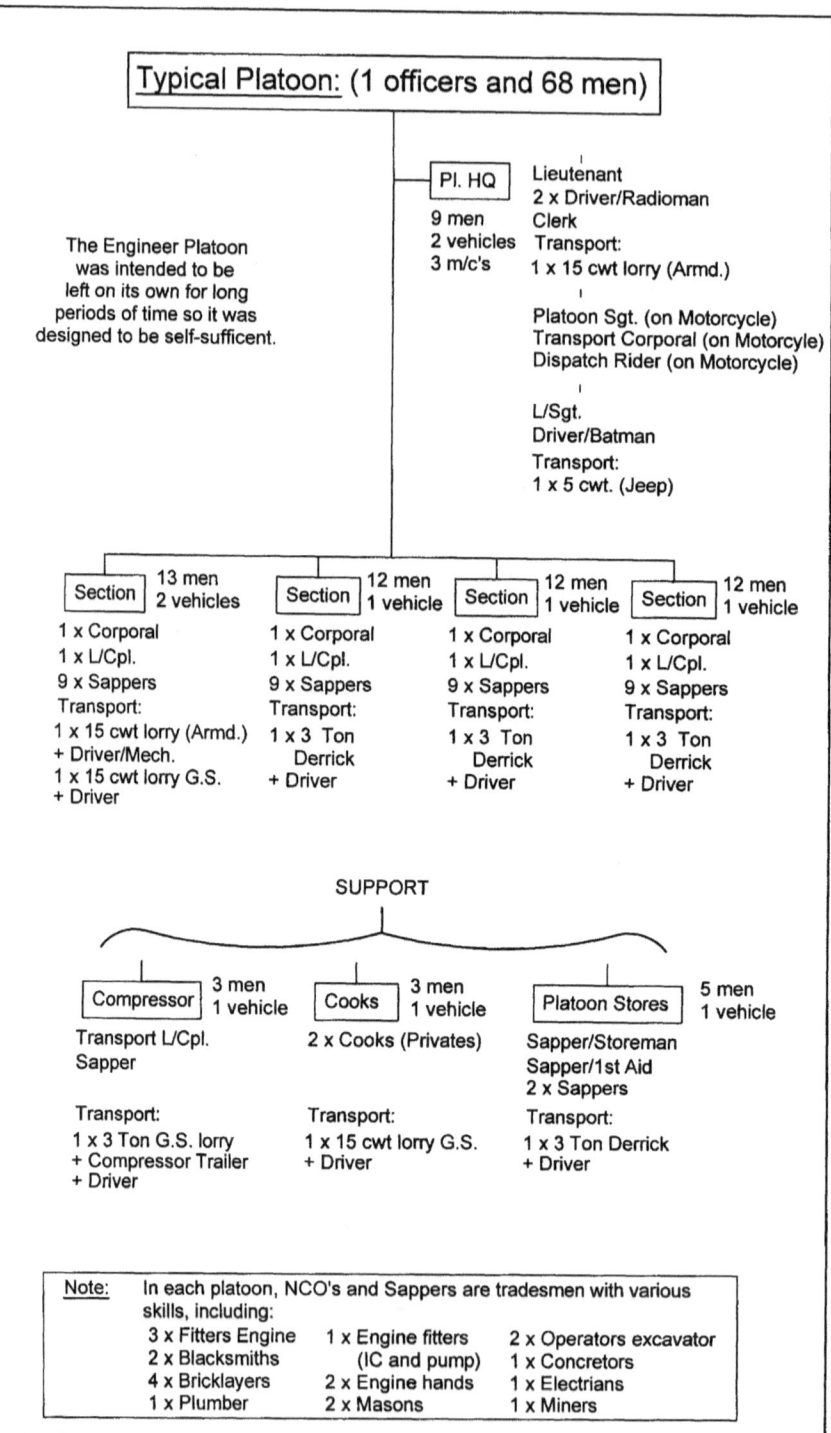

Typical Platoon: (1 officers and 68 men)

The Engineer Platoon was intended to be left on its own for long periods of time so it was designed to be self-sufficent.

Pl. HQ
9 men
2 vehicles
3 m/c's

Lieutenant
2 x Driver/Radioman
Clerk
Transport:
1 x 15 cwt lorry (Armd.)

Platoon Sgt. (on Motorcycle)
Transport Corporal (on Motorcyle)
Dispatch Rider (on Motorcycle)

L/Sgt.
Driver/Batman
Transport:
1 x 5 cwt. (Jeep)

Section — 13 men, 2 vehicles
1 x Corporal
1 x L/Cpl.
9 x Sappers
Transport:
1 x 15 cwt lorry (Armd.)
+ Driver/Mech.
1 x 15 cwt lorry G.S.
+ Driver

Section — 12 men, 1 vehicle
1 x Corporal
1 x L/Cpl.
9 x Sappers
Transport:
1 x 3 Ton
    Derrick
+ Driver

Section — 12 men, 1 vehicle
1 x Corporal
1 x L/Cpl.
9 x Sappers
Transport:
1 x 3 Ton
    Derrick
+ Driver

Section — 12 men, 1 vehicle
1 x Corporal
1 x L/Cpl.
9 x Sappers
Transport:
1 x 3 Ton
    Derrick
+ Driver

SUPPORT

Compressor — 3 men, 1 vehicle
Transport L/Cpl.
Sapper

Transport:
1 x 3 Ton G.S. lorry
+ Compressor Trailer
+ Driver

Cooks — 3 men, 1 vehicle
2 x Cooks (Privates)

Transport:
1 x 15 cwt lorry G.S.
+ Driver

Platoon Stores — 5 men, 1 vehicle
Sapper/Storeman
Sapper/1st Aid
2 x Sappers
Transport:
1 x 3 Ton Derrick
+ Driver

Note:	In each platoon, NCO's and Sappers are tradesmen with various skills, including:		
	3 x Fitters Engine	1 x Engine fitters	2 x Operators excavator
	2 x Blacksmiths	(IC and pump)	1 x Concretors
	4 x Bricklayers	2 x Engine hands	1 x Electrians
	1 x Plumber	2 x Masons	1 x Miners

Above: Lieutenant James Russel Martin. (Russ Kennedy)

were sent back to Brockville to serve as instructors. They were posted to the 23rd in early 1943, which was then being formed in New Brunswick, for overseas deployment. Each lieutenant was put in charge of a platoon; Kennedy the 2nd, while Martin took over the 3rd.

After a temporary posting to the 7th Canadian Infantry Division, which was responsible during the war for the defense of Eastern Canada, the 23rd Field Company, Royal Canadian Engineers boarded the S.S. Pasteur and sailed for England on July 16th 1943. They arrived in England on July 22nd and were stationed at Wentworth Hall. Nine days later they were transferred to 1st Canadian Army Troop, Royal Canadian Engineers, under the command of Lieutenant-Colonel N.I. Fraser. In January 1944 the 23rd Field Company, Royal Canadian Engineers went to Ripon to receive further training and instruction at the School of Military Engineering. Then, on March 17th, they were sent to practice their Assault Tidal Crossing techniques on the Trent and Ouse Rivers, an area with high tides and plenty of thick mud. The lessons that they learned there would prove to be invaluable during Operation Berlin. On April 2nd they saw Storm boats for the first time. Their unit history, *The Twenty-Third Story* commented on this new piece of equipment that was still considered to be experimental: "[Storm boats] *are a new piece of equipment of American origin.* They are made of plywood and are designed to carry twelve to sixteen fully equipped men. They are powered by 50 H.P. Evinrude out-board motors. The motors are very powerful, but we find them most unreliable, except under very favourable conditions. Since none of us has seen such a boat before, our handling of them at first is pretty awful, but we do improve.*" [6]

The 1st Platoon was selected to train in operating them while the other platoons concentrated on bridging open water. On the 28th it was time to put their training into practice during the first of the 'Kate' exercises, the purpose of which was for them to support The Royal Regiment of Canada's assault cross-

* They were mistaken. The boats were of British design while the motor was American. See my book, *Allied Attack Boats*, which explains in detail the differences between US and British made Storm boats and Assault boats.

Above: Major Mike Tucker in October 1944, CO of the 23rd all through the unit's North West European Campaign. (Russ Kennedy)

ing of the Trent River. It turned out to be a poorly coordinated affair and was only successful in getting the Royals across the river. Difficulties arose when a battalion of the Essex Scottish, who were providing the carrying parties for the cumbersome boats, were so poorly controlled that the members of the 23rd Field Company, RCE had to abandon their tasks to lend a hand in an attempt to keep to the schedule. Additionally, the company experienced for the first time just how temperamental the engines on the Storm boats were. Only fifty percent of the boats assigned to the first wave actually made it across the river. *The Twenty-Third Story* records their poor performance. *"We shall have to do better than this on operations."* [7]

The second "Kate" exercise was more complex and successful. This exercise involved not only ferrying a battalion of The Royal Highlanders of Canada across the Trent, but also transporting all their equipment. This equipment included seventeen jeeps, six 6-pounder anti-tank guns and 1200 pounds of ammunition, all moved by the company's Storm boats. A third "Kate" exercise included the 23rd Field Company, RCE training an infantry battalion, this time the Essex Scottish, in the art of moving Storm boats from their transport vehicles to the water and then themselves into the boats. The fourth "Kate" exercise was used to refine the 23rd's skills in the use of its new assault crossing capability. After all of this specialty training, it was clear to the members of the 23rd that they were destined to carry out an assault crossing on one of the great rivers of Europe.

Despite this specialty training, the many months spent in the field on the Kate exercises had eroded the unit's morale, to the point where the army felt that a change of command was needed. This came in the form of Major Michael L. Tucker, DSO (1907-1981) from Montreal, Quebec. In his privately published diary, *Whispers and Shadows*, Lt. Russ Kennedy stated that Major Tucker *"led us into France through the N.W. Europe campaign and back to England with dash and style, with unvarying fairness and with a judicious mixture of firmness and fatherly concern."* [8] Others, like sappers Clayton Moss, Stan Goodall and Willie Richardson, have also commented on how well they

Above: Five officers on leave in the UK. Back l to r: George Reynolds, James Russ Martin and Russ Kennedy. Front row l to r: Lt. Hugh Millward and Stewart Smith. (Russ Kennedy)

Below: No. 2 Platoon in the UK. Lt. Kennedy is second from the left in the front row. The platoon Sergeant and several of the men weren't present. Russ describes the L/Sgt. to his right as a very capable tobacco-chewing mason-contractor from west of Toronto. (Russ Kennedy)

admired the way that their new commanding officer (CO) ran the company. The general consensus was that he was consistently fair. On a whole, the change was a big boost to morale. Major Tucker even made an impression on famed Canadian writer and Arnhem survivor, Leo Heaps, who wrote many books, including several on the Arnhem battle and on what happened to the men left behind that became evaders. In his book 'The Grey Goose of Arnhem' Heaps described Mike Tucker as, *"square-built, slow-talking Tucker who no one could hurry. He was a dedicated man, an arch conservative in the private life who upheld the order of past things. But in battle he would try anything once."* [9]

On the 5th of July the 23rd Field Company, RCE started to prepare to go to France and by the 14th they were working in Caen, helping to clear the city of debris left from battle and bombing. In mid-July 1944 most of Caen was flattened by Allied bombers and in many places it was difficult to discern where the street had been. It was decided that the new road would go through the centre of the town and down to the Orne River. The only problem was that the Germans still held the south bank. Lieutenant Russ Kennedy in his diary remembered, *"Here we were subject to some mortar and artillery fire and the odd bomb run by German air, but were not in too much danger as long as we took all the precautions we had been trained to do."* [10]

This wasn't the first time that the unit had been under fire. A few days earlier they were repairing roads in Cairon when they were caught between a Canadian battery firing from behind them and a German battery in front. Shells from both sides were screaming over them as they worked. They quickly learned that if you heard a bang before the scream of the shell, there was nothing to fear, as it was coming from the Canadian battery. However, if you only heard the scream then they had to get down because it had 'Made In Germany' on it. Luckily, no one was hurt in the incident. Under the eyes of the enemy, the members of ICAT, RCE plowed directly through the rubble and wrecked buildings of Caen to create a new road. On August 4th, this dirt road was opened and named 'Andy's Alley' after Lt. A.B. Anderson of HQ RCE, ICAT. It is now called 'la rue 6 Juin'.

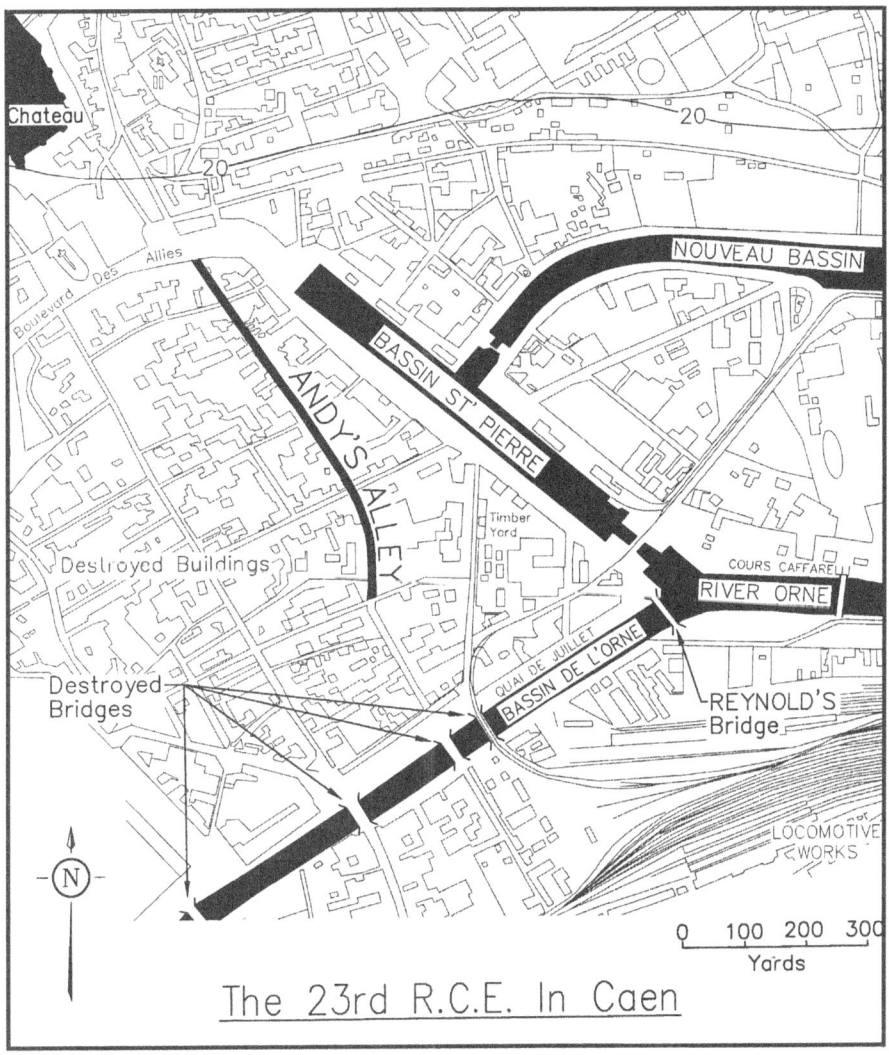

The 23rd R.C.E. In Caen

During this time, they built a 150 foot (45.72M) Bailey Bridge over the Orne River and named it Reynold's Bridge, after the unit's first war casualty. Captain George Reynold had been killed in a demolition accident on July 23rd. This was the start of an unfortunate pattern, as Lieutenant Kennedy explained: *"The second-in-command was in charge of the company office and every time they got bored and left, something bad always happened to them.* George Reynolds was observing the demolition of the buildings in Caen when he was killed. Some men thought that he*

* = Captain Don McIntryre replaced him. Fortunately, his boredom induced mishap that happened several months later wasn't fatal. He was only wounded when he strayed from his office during Pegasus II.

17

Above: Reynolds Bridge in Caen. Photo taken by Michael Dean on July 29th, 1944. (Library and Archives of Canada PA-116511)

Below: Major Tucker poses at the bridge named after his fallen second in command.

Two photographs taken by Ken Bell on August 4th, 1944.
Above: Sergeant W.G. Willick reflecting on the damage done to the city of Caen.
(PA-114504 Library and Archives of Canada)
Below: Grader at work on Andy's Alley, a new street built by ICAT in Caen,
through the wrecked buildings and rubble. It was 1/2 mile long and took 5 days
to complete. (PA-190015 Library and Archives of Canada)

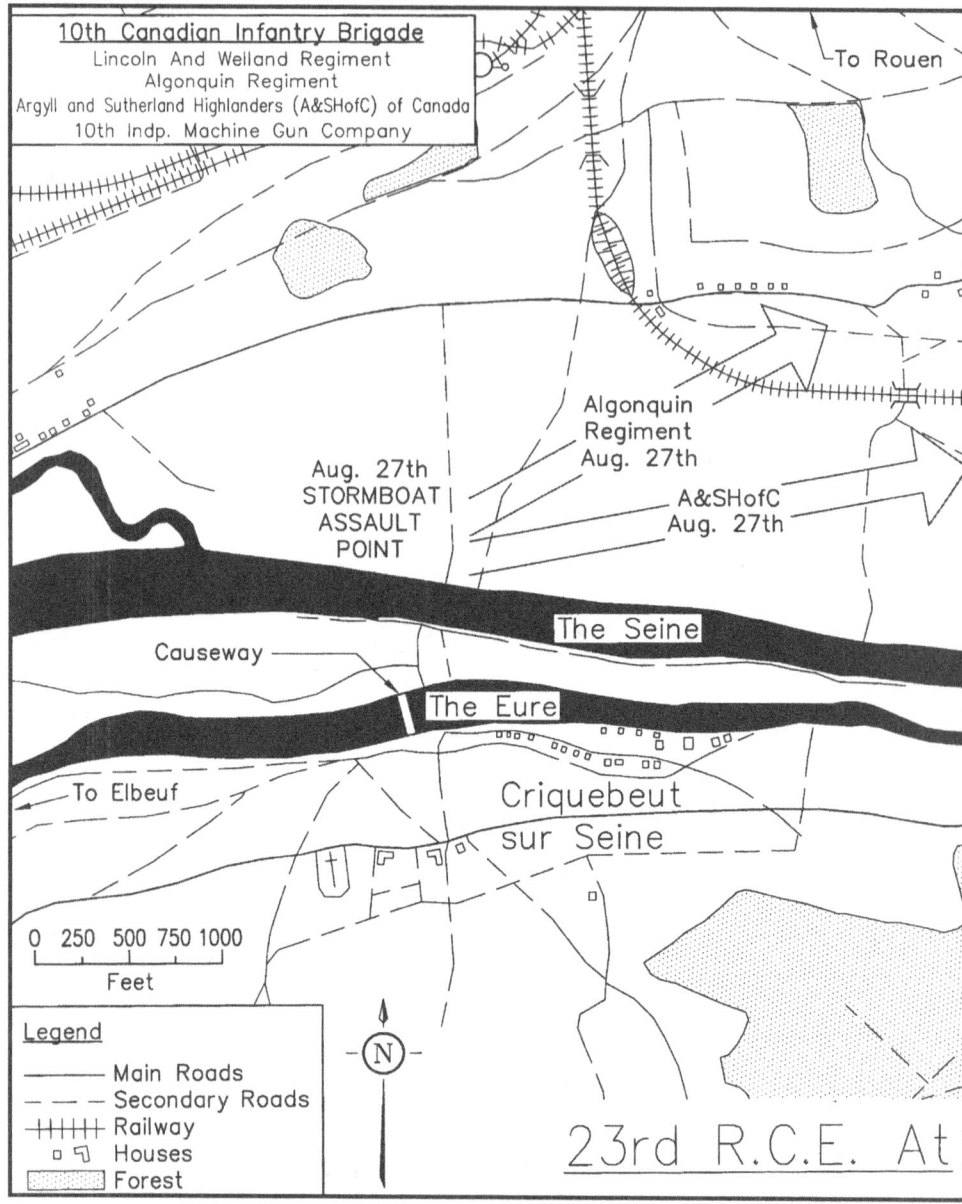

10th Canadian Infantry Brigade
Lincoln And Welland Regiment
Algonquin Regiment
Argyll and Sutherland Highlanders (A&SHofC) of Canada
10th Indp. Machine Gun Company

To Rouen

Algonquin
Regiment
Aug. 27th

Aug. 27th
STORMBOAT
ASSAULT
POINT

A&SHofC
Aug. 27th

The Seine

Causeway

The Eure

To Elbeuf

Criquebeut
sur Seine

0 250 500 750 1000
Feet

Legend
——— Main Roads
– – – Secondary Roads
++++++ Railway
□ ⌐ Houses
▨▨▨ Forest

-(N)-

23rd R.C.E. At

was killed by a sniper. Major Tucker was so distressed by George's death that he asked me to be at his autopsy. I concluded that a piece of the PIAT round that the guys were using to bring down some of the more dangerous buildings came back and hit George in the forehead." [11]

Previously, the sappers had asked if they could use the PIAT bombs on the unstable structures instead of having to go in them to plant charges. Permission was granted as no one could find

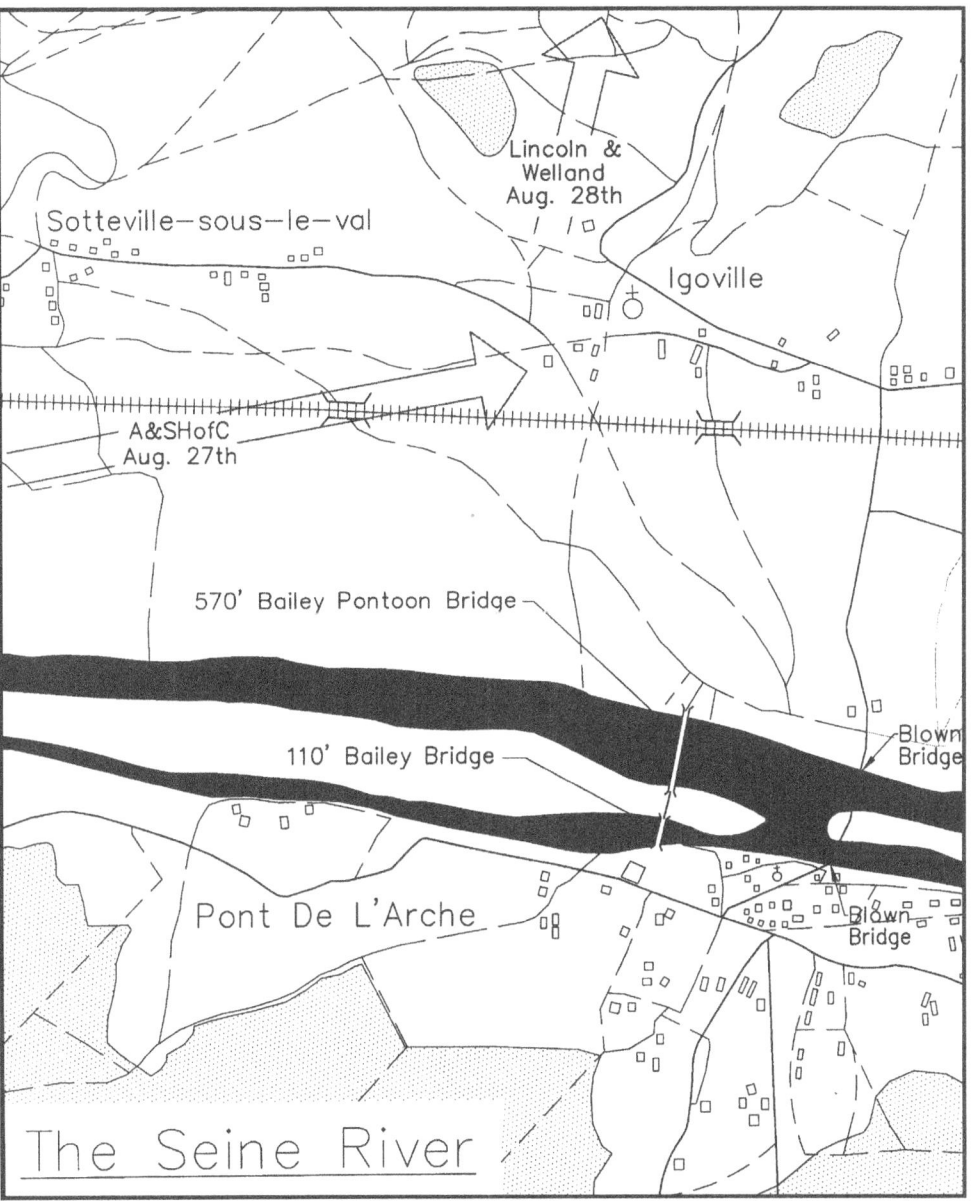

Lincoln &
Welland
Aug. 28th

Sotteville—sous—le—val

Igoville

A&SHofC
Aug. 27th

570' Bailey Pontoon Bridge

110' Bailey Bridge

Blown
Bridge

Pont De L'Arche

Blown
Bridge

The Seine River

another use for the bombs. These weapons were on the company's equipment list and were meant to be used in case they found themselves in the way of an enemy armoured assault.

Twenty-three days later, on a clear day, the 23rd Field Company, RCE used twenty Storm boats to ferry two battalions of the 10th Infantry Brigade (of the Canadian 4th Armored Division) across the Seine River at Criquebeuf-sur-Seine. Despite being shelled, the 23rd were so efficient in their ferrying duties that the infantry never had to wait for a boat. In fact, the follow-up companies marched straight to the river and onto the waiting boats. Still, the crossing at Criquebeuf wasn't without drama. The boats didn't arrive until 0400 hours and it was decided that the only way for the boats to be ready in time was to drive the equipment `as loaded for transport' with three boats stacked per truck rather than `tactically' with one boat and one motor per truck, as preferred. With the Germans holding the high ground on the other side of the river, it was imperative that the boats were put in position under the cover of darkness. *The Twenty-Third Story* comments on the drive: *"It is a long tortuous drive through the black aisles of the forest leading down to the river, but when we come into the open, near the river bank, it is growing light. We are warned by the troops holding Criquebeuf that the whole area is under observation by the Germans, occupying the high ground a thousand yards away across the river, and that it is suicidal to go with the operation."* [12] When the trucks rolled across the causeway and parked amongst the trees next to the beach, they were noticed. German artillery opened up, mostly pounding the causeway where the trucks had passed. Fortunately, our own artillery launched a counter-battery shoot and put an end to the heavy barrage. Still, shells landed in the area during the operation, but only two sappers from the 23rd were wounded. Sapper G.P. Perkins remained with the unit, but Sapper C.T. Nogueira's wounds were just serious enough for him to be evacuated to the hospital. Lieutenant Kennedy summed up the Seine crossing from the 23rd Field Company, RCE's point of view: *"The first platoon of the Algonquins appeared and from then on we had a beautiful tidy operation."*[13]

Unfortunately for the infantry, the crossing was the smoothest part of the operation. The 10th Infantry Brigade lost a number of men when it tried to expand their bridgehead and capture the high ground. With only small boats operating on the river, they were fighting without any heavy equipment which was waiting for larger crafts to bring it across. To rectify this problem, the next day the 23rd operated two Class 40 rafts at the same spot on the river to ferry the tanks of the Canadian 4th

Above: The Seine Bridge looking from the island. It was capable of taking the weight of most Allied tanks and vehicles. (Bob Tate)

Top Inset: Lt. Bob Tate wrote on the back of this photo, `The Seine Bridge. What a length. Near here was the T.T.C. ferry.' (Bob Tate)

Bottom Inset: one of the Class 40 rafts that the company used on the Seine River. (Bob Tate)

Armoured Division across. These rafts were basically a section of bridging that was supported by two large pontoon piers, just strong enough to transport a Sherman tank across a river. During this operation, two more sappers were wounded, but neither seriously. Sappers W. Collins and J. Tinant were sent to hospital.

Their last task on the Seine River was to build a floating bridge in less than twenty-four hours. It was built upstream at Pont de l'Arche and while the project was still under the command of Major Tucker, it involved the entire ICAT, RCE.* Again, this task didn't go without its share of drama, though this incident ended on a humorous note. *The Twenty-Third Story's* recorded the event: *"It is almost certain that a bridge will be required at Pont de l'Arche, so a recce party goes out in the evening to look for a suitable site. They observe due precautions going down to the river and whilst they are looking around, but they grow careless, and are apparently seen coming away. Then and there they are treated to a first-class mortar stonk by the Germans. When it becomes apparent that the enemy is going to take the whole thing seriously, they desert the meager protection of the gutters along the street and seek shelter in a basement. The Hun entertains them with a full forty-five minutes of plain and fancy mortaring. Many hits are scored on the building in which they have taken refuge, and they breathe a sigh of relief when the performance is ended and they are safely back in camp."* [14]

This account failed to record that the recce party consisted of a bored Major Tucker and his jeepless recce officer. Lieutenant Kennedy's jeep was in for repairs and when he asked for another vehicle Major Tucker informed him that *"there's my jeep,"* then he grinned slyly, *"and I'll drive it!"* The "precautions" that they had taken to get down to the river was to literally crawl on the hard cobblestones. On the way back, they got tired of hurting their knees so they got `careless'. In Lieutenant Kennedy's words, *"One of us said, `There isn't a German within miles.' We both stood up and started walking. Mistake. We heard the mor-*

---

* = The 5th Field Company constructed the 110 foot (33.52M) Bailey Bridge over the Eura river as well as helping with the main bridge. The 20th built the far loading bays, two additional bays and the anti-mine boom.

Above: the recce party. Major Tucker is at the wheel as he and Lt. Kennedy pose for a photo at a recently cleared German road-block in Abbeville. The vertical logs are what is left of the road-block. (Russ Kennedy)

Below: Bob Tate wrote on the back of this photograph, `A road block in Abbeville. All the streets on the north side of the Somme were like this.' (Bob Tate)

tars coming and hit the cobbles." They found a basement to hide in and when the shelling finally stopped, they came out and they saw that the jeep had been destroyed. They had to walk five or six kilometers back to the unit. *"Neither of us referred to the incident again,"* remembered Lieutenant Kennedy, *"and I don't suppose that it was reported to higher authority in any detail."* [15]

The unit was next tasked with strengthening the bridges over the Somme at Abbeville. This mission attracted the attention of the Chief Engineer of the II Corps, Brigadier General Walsh, who was very satisfied with how quickly and efficiently the work on the two bridges was executed. From there the 23rd moved onto St. Omer to further support the advance of the II Canadian Corps by repairing roads damaged by the German retreat. One such road was near a V-1 flying bomb launching site and was badly cratered by misfired bombs. It was quickly patched up and made useable. Some damaged parts from the launching site were used as fill for the larger craters.

On 16th September, the 23rd found themselves racing to Bourg -Leopold to be part of the Special Bridging Force under the command of the British XXX Corps. They arrived at 3 a.m. on the 17th after driving approximately 200 miles to get there. The official War Diary states for the 16th September 1944: *"The unit left its location near St. Omer at 0745 hrs and moved via BETHUNE and LENS into Belgium at 25 miles in 2 hrs. The coy. Arrived in BRUSSELS at approximately 1500 hrs (120 miles from ST. OMER) but due to the heavy traffic welcome given the coy. while in the city impressed all personnel. The convoy was met by Major Tucker and Lt. Kennedy on the eastern outskirts of the city at approximately 2030 hrs. The column then drove a further 50 miles before stopping for a rest.* [16]

It took more than two hours to get through Brussels because all the newly liberated Belgians were celebrating in the streets. The men of the 23rd received the standard greeting of gifts of fruit and wine. Their unit history states about the party in the Belgium capital: *"We are thrilled to the core and looked forward to making camp and joining in the celebration,"* [17] in the Belgian capital.

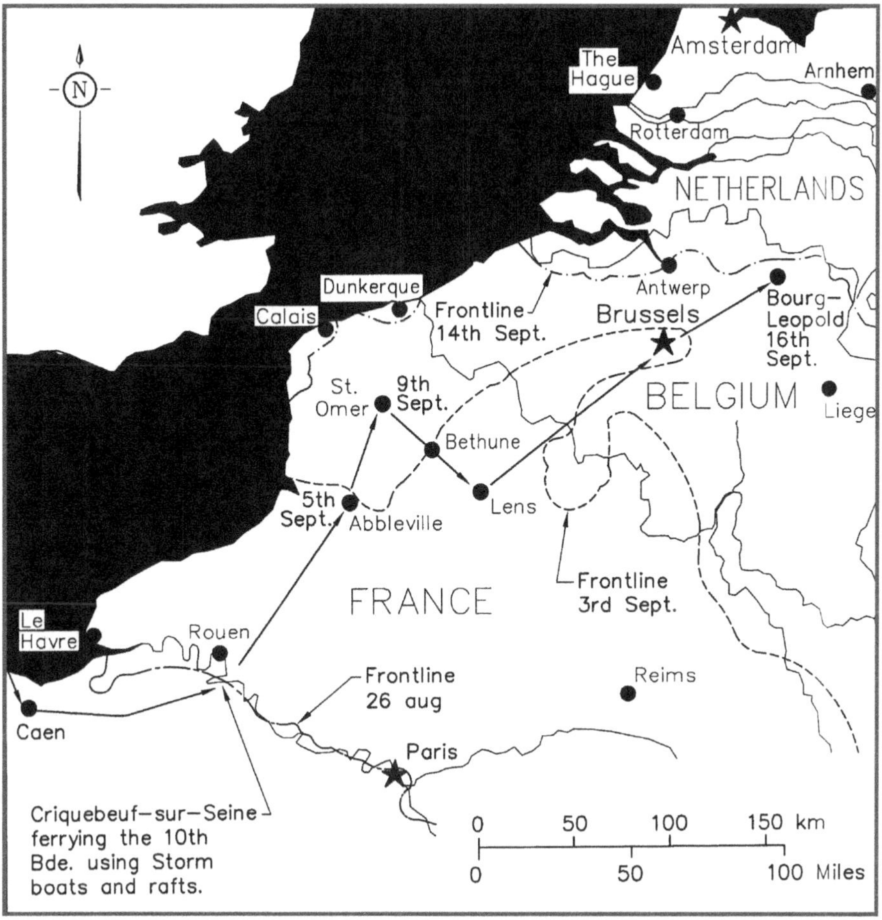

The Route of the 23rd to September 16th 1944

Right: one of the three Panthers left behind in the flight over the Seine River at Pont de l'Arche, August 1944. (Bob Tate)

Unfortunately, this wasn't to be. The company received orders to continue on to Hechtel, the staging area for the bridging force, so there was to be no party for the 23rd. The War Diary for Septmeber 17th summarized the move as follows: *"The Company halted from 0300 hrs to 0730 hrs about 1 mile south of the ALBERT CANAL AT BR 320625 (Brussels-Liege Sheet) and Major Tucker and Lt. Kennedy returned to Brussels to guide 10 Cdn Field Park Company to the new area. 23 Cdn. Field Company crossed the ALBERT CANAL via a Bailey Pontoon bridge and halted again just north of the canal until approx. 1030 hrs., before being guided to the formation area near HECHTEL at BR 360875 (BRUSSELS-LIEGE Sheet). The unit rested for the remainder of the day. The total distance of the move was just over 200 miles'.*[18]

The unit pulled into an orchard to get some rest and here they were ambushed by throngs of celebrating Belgians who bombarded them with presents of eggs, tomatoes and fruit. "Ain't war *grand."* [19], was how Major Tucker summed up this `attack' on his troops. Even after succumbing to this assault, they were in position and prepared for whatever mission lay ahead, though not one sapper had any idea what that would be. No one did. However, they were confident that their well trained and experienced unit was ready to make a difference in whatever task they were to be assigned.

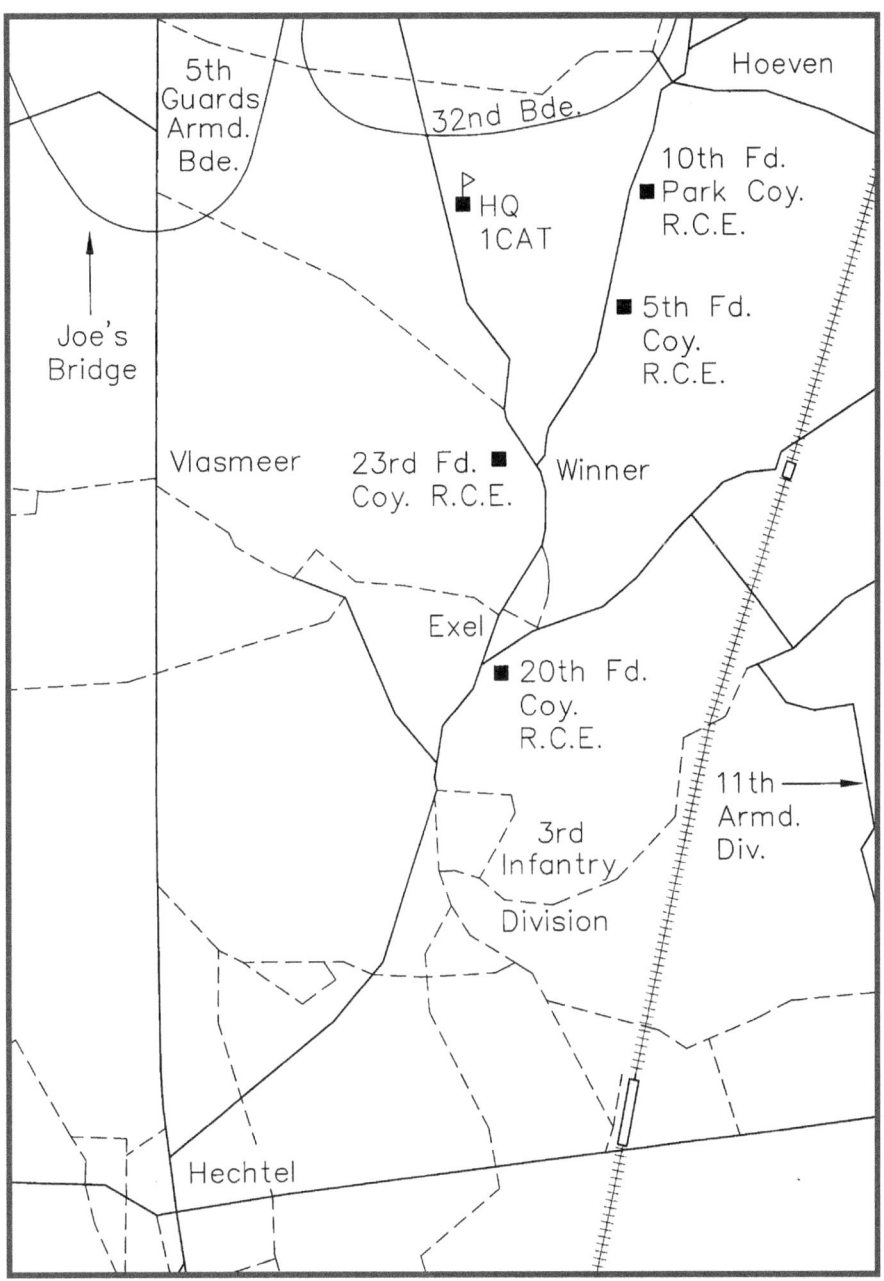

ICAT's Unit Positions September 17th

The Origins of the Storm Boat MK 1

Before the start of the Second World War, the German Army had pioneered the concept of an assault boat powered by an outboard motor that would quickly allow soldiers to cross water obstacles. Not only did the outboard motor allow for a rapid river crossing where speed and surprise were crucial, but it made crossing rivers whose currents were previously too strong for paddle powered rubber dinghies possible. The German Army had developed the storm boats, which they officially designated

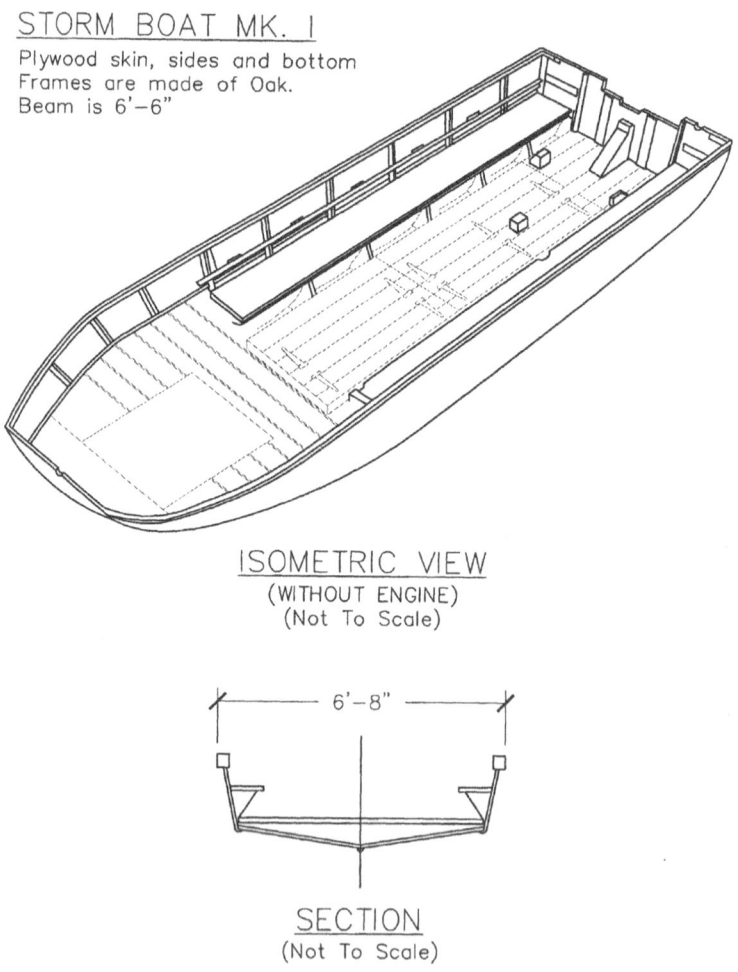

STORM BOAT MK. I
Plywood skin, sides and bottom
Frames are made of Oak.
Beam is 6'-6"

ISOMETRIC VIEW
(WITHOUT ENGINE)
(Not To Scale)

6'-8"

SECTION
(Not To Scale)

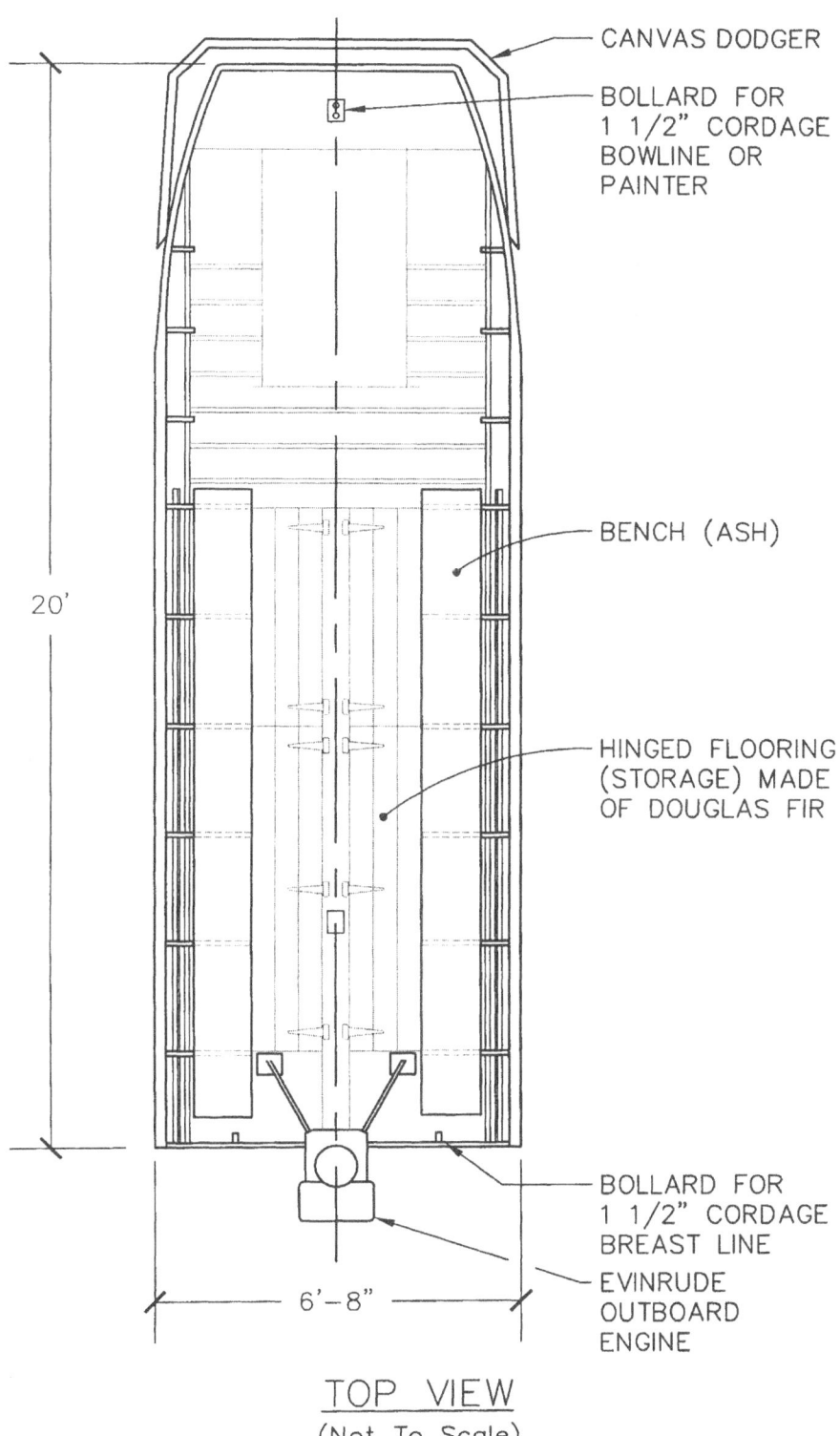

CANVAS DODGER

BOLLARD FOR
1 1/2" CORDAGE
BOWLINE OR
PAINTER

BENCH (ASH)

HINGED FLOORING
(STORAGE) MADE
OF DOUGLAS FIR

20'

6'-8"

BOLLARD FOR
1 1/2" CORDAGE
BREAST LINE

EVINRUDE
OUTBOARD
ENGINE

TOP VIEW
(Not To Scale)

31

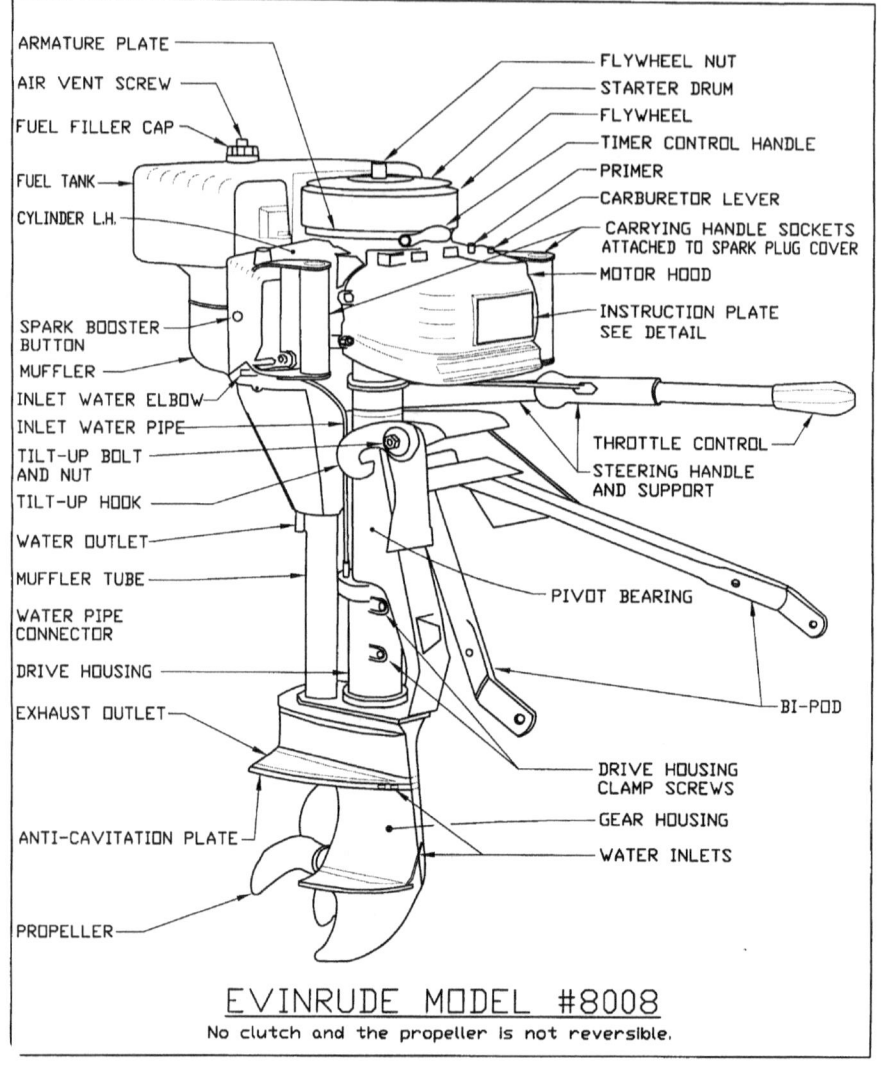

ARMATURE PLATE
AIR VENT SCREW
FUEL FILLER CAP
FUEL TANK
CYLINDER L.H.
SPARK BOOSTER BUTTON
MUFFLER
INLET WATER ELBOW
INLET WATER PIPE
TILT-UP BOLT AND NUT
TILT-UP HOOK
WATER OUTLET
MUFFLER TUBE
WATER PIPE CONNECTOR
DRIVE HOUSING
EXHAUST OUTLET
ANTI-CAVITATION PLATE
PROPELLER

FLYWHEEL NUT
STARTER DRUM
FLYWHEEL
TIMER CONTROL HANDLE
PRIMER
CARBURETOR LEVER
CARRYING HANDLE SOCKETS ATTACHED TO SPARK PLUG COVER
MOTOR HOOD
INSTRUCTION PLATE SEE DETAIL
THROTTLE CONTROL
STEERING HANDLE AND SUPPORT
PIVOT BEARING
BI-POD
DRIVE HOUSING CLAMP SCREWS
GEAR HOUSING
WATER INLETS

EVINRUDE MODEL #8008
No clutch and the propeller is not reversible.

INSTRUCTIONS

1. MIX ONE PINT #50 OIL WITH EACH GALLON OF GASOLINE, BEFORE FILLING TANK.
2. OPEN VENT SCREW (ON TANK CAP).
3. OPEN GAS COCK UNDER TANK (TOWARD YOU).
4. SET CARBURETOR LEVER TO COLD.
5. SET TIMER TO START.
6. SET STEERING GRIP TO START.
7. WRAP ROPE ON FLYWHEEL.
8. PUSH PRIMER FIVE TIMES.
9. SPIN FLYWHEEL WITH STRONG PULLS
10. WHEN STARTED MOVE TIMER AT ONCE TO RUN, ALSO TURN STEERING GRIP TOWARD FAST.
11. WITH THROTTLE WIDE OPEN ADJUST CARB. LEVER TOWARD WARM UNTIL MOTOR RUNS SMOOTHLY.
12. IF MOTOR IS HOT PRIME SPARINGLY.
13. STOP MOTOR BY MOVING TIMER HANDLE ALL THE WAY TO LEFT.
14. USE CHAMPION R-7 SPARK PLUGS.

EVINRUDE MOTOR, MILWAUKEE, WIS., U.S.A.

INSTRUCTION PLATE DETAIL

Sturmboot "39" (the model number was in reference to the year it was adopted by the army), or "Blitz" boats, specifically to cross the Rhine River as a way to breach French defenses. This they successfully achieved at Colmar, along the Franco-German border on 15 June 1940.

The French defenders would have had little idea of what was racing towards them as the Germans had intentionally kept this piece of engineering equipment from being observed prior to the war. Even though an effective artillery barrage had shelled the French positions for 10 minutes, the initial resistance to the assault left more than one-half of the Sturmboots out of service, some due to malfunctioning motors. However, after the successful piercing of the French defenses at Colmar, Sturmboots were used in all theatres of war where the German army needed to quickly establish a bridgehead over a fast flowing river. Photographic evidence exists of German engineers employing the Sturmboots in Scandinavia, Russia, Yugoslavia and even the defensive battles of Western Europe of 1944.

The German Sturmboots were constructed from plywood, 19'-9" long and 5'-2" across the beam. They had the capacity to carry eight fully equipped soldiers, plus a crew of one. Additional assistance was needed from the engineer company, as it took eight men to carry the boat and four to carry the motor. The 40-horse power motor was purpose-built with a long propeller shaft, which was used as a rudder to steer the craft. This allowed the Sturmboot to reach speeds of 16 knots. The Germans, much like the British later, grouped these boats into special Sturmboot companies, whose only tasks were to transport, maintain and operate these boats.

Like other new concepts of warfare introduced by the Germans, the British, to support their own combat engineering needs, expropriated the Sturmboot idea. The purpose for the boats was identical to the German use; to quickly transport combat troops over a wide, fast river during opposed crossings. The Storm boats were developed at the Experimental Bridging Establishment at Christchurch Barracks in the United Kingdom. There the boats were not just replicated, but improved to fit British tactical requirements. This involved changing the dimensions of the craft to accommodate a jeep or a 6-pound anti-tank gun to be ferried on the boats. This would allow for the securing of a stronger bridgehead, to better deflect an armoured counter-attack. Much like the German model, the British boats were made out of plywood, however, seat tracks or benches were made out of oak, and were fitted along the sides. These could be used not only as seats for the soldiers but also as a platform for either the jeep or the gun. To accommodate for the benches, the beam (width) of the British version was increased to 6'-6", over a foot wider than the German version, although there was only a marginal increase of 3" in the boat's length to 20 feet. To facilitate the loading of a jeep or gun, the bow was considerably flatter than the German model and a set of ramps were provided so either piece of equipment could be rolled up onto the seat tracks. An unforeseen consequence of improving the boat's tactical capabilities for the British Army was that the weight of the boats increased. It was not possible for twelve men to carry the Storm boat, as it was for the German version, but 16 to 18 men were needed to manhandle the 900 pound British model. This increase in weight was to affect operations on the night of 25/26 September 1944.

The motor that propelled the Storm boat was the American made Evinrude, model #8008 outboard engine, originally designed for the commercial pre-war recreational market. It was a 198-pound, 50-horsepower, 2-stroke engine. The motor sat on the stern transom and on the apex of an A-frame, to which legs were attached inside the boat. This arrangement allowed for the motor to be quickly brought on board if necessary. The vertical shaft was hinged on the transom bracket so that the motor tilted on striking the riverbed in shallow water. It had a three and a half gallon fuel tank with four additional fuel cans stored under the seat tracks. This was necessary because at full speed the engine would consume 4 to 5 gallons of fuel per hour. The engine did not have a clutch or reverse gear, however, it was able to turn with a 90-degree steering angle. The Evinrude model #8008 had been adopted partially due to the Hyde Park Declaration of

1941 between Canada and the U.S.A. This agreement stated that each country should provide the other with munitions and equipment, which it was best able to produce. This engine had already been adopted by the U.S. Army Engineer Corps to propel their infantry boats, so it was duly taken on both Canada's and Britain's inventory.

There was, however, a very strong drawback to adopting this civilian engine for military use. It was prone to suddenly stopping when the spark plugs became wet. This may not have been much of an issue for recreational boaters on warm, sunny days, but under the conditions that the engineers demanded it to perform the sudden and unexpected cessation of all power could have deadly consequences. It was not until October 1944, with the experience of the evacuation still very fresh in their memories, that the 23rd Field Company, RCE was able to modify their engines to prevent them from failing. On 26 October 1944, one month to the day since the unit was in action on the Lower Rhine, Colonel C.J. Bermingham, OC of the 1st Canadian Army Group Royal Engineers (1CAGRE), was presented with a report on how to waterproof the Evinrude engines. In a report entitled *Waterproofing and Modification of the Evinrude Outboard Motor* it was found that if the motors were not waterproofed, only 50% would start in wet conditions but if waterproofed this jumped to a 90% start rate. Also, the effects of a wave over the stern had no effect on the modified engines, while the untreated engines would stall and not start again until they dried out.

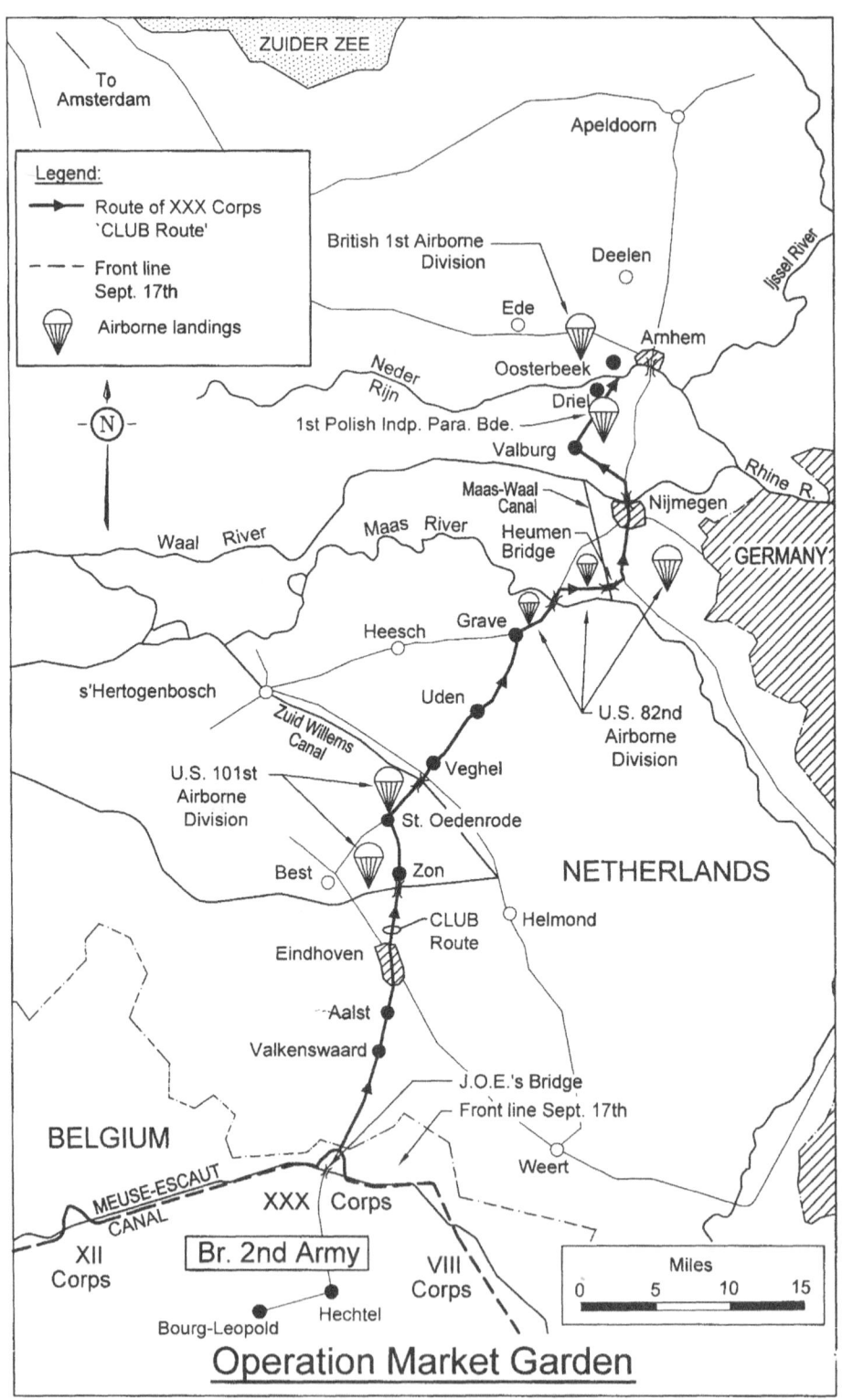

Operation Market Garden

Operation Market Garden

Operation Market Garden: The Plan

It is not the objective of this book to provide a detailed account of the battles that were fought during Operation Market Garden. Nor do the underlying political and strategic considerations which necessitated Market Garden figure greatly into the account of the actions of the 23rd Field Company, RCE. However, some mention of the events in Western Europe during the summer of 1944 is necessary.

After the breakout from Normandy and the rush to Germany, General Eisenhower accepted Field Marshal Montgomery's plan to employ the 1st Allied Airborne Army in a daring operation that would exploit the chaotic situation created by the retreating German Army. The plan, Operation Market Garden, envisioned the 1st Airborne Army and the British 2nd Army punching a hole in the weak German lines and opening a clear path all the way to Berlin. To achieve this, three airborne divisions (a total of 35,000 men and their equipment) were supposed to seize all the bridges along the way. (See map on the opposite page). This airborne spearhead would pave the way for the British XXX Corps and the rest of the British 2nd Army to drive north and swing left into the industrial heart of Germany, the Ruhr valley. It was expected that the Germans would be caught in such disarray, after their rapid withdrawal from France and Belgium, as to allow the airborne units to be quickly relieved by XXX Corps as it headed on to the Ruhr. Considering that two German armies had just been destroyed in Normandy and that the remaining Germans forces were in a state of chaos, this plan had the potential to put the final nail in Hitler's coffin. It would be like battles of old, with the cavalry exploiting the newly created gap in the enemy line.

Unfortunately, many factors were working against the Allies. A major problem was that there weren't enough aircraft to bring in all 35,000 men in one lift; it would require three lifts over three days. Further, the weather caused many delays for the follow-up lifts, which hindered operations, as well as preventing tactical air support. Finally the swift and unexpectedly strong recovery of the German forces created a situation that caught Allied commanders off guard. Other factors contributed to the negative outcome of the battle and have been the source of considerable debate ever since. The combination of risks that had been calculated for and unforeseen events doomed Market Garden to failure and set the scene for a daring rescue across the swift and dangerous currents of the Neder Rijn.

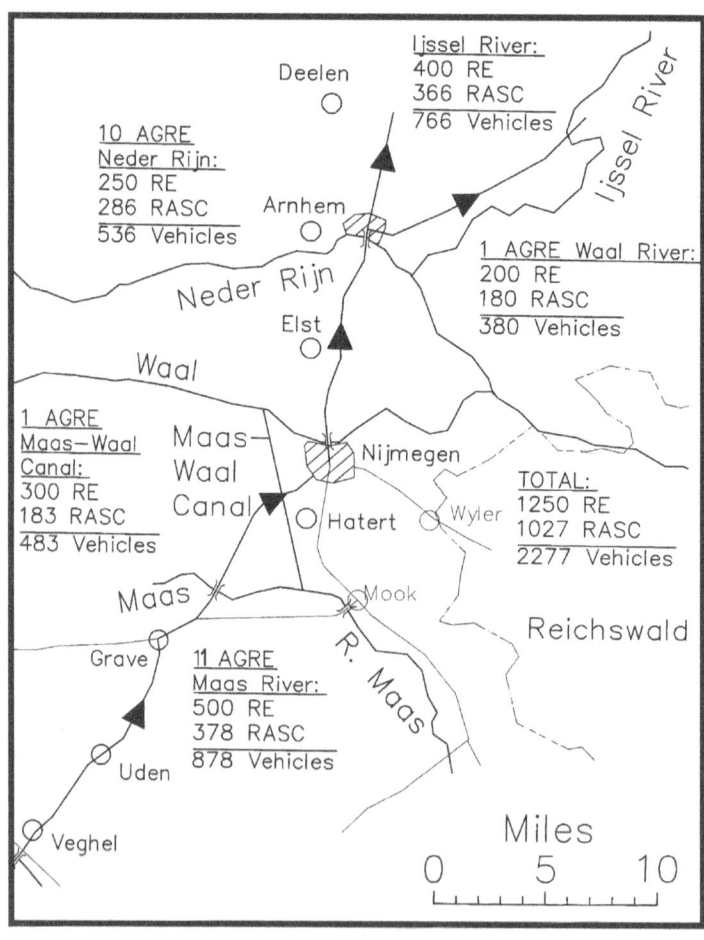

Planned Deployment for Simultaneous Duties

The Plan of the Special Bridging Force

Although both the airborne and ground elements of Operation Market Garden were plagued with an unwarranted sense of optimism, certain safeguards were put into place. To minimize the very real possibility that the airborne element would not capture all the bridges intact, The British Second Army created the Special Bridging Force (SBF) to ensure that XXX Corps would not be delayed from its final objective; crossing the Neder Rijn. The force had enough men and equipment to bridge all of the water obstacles it would encounter. The plan called for the airborne divisions to capture bridges over three rivers; the Waal, the Maas and the Neder Rijn and three canals; the Wilhelmina, the Zuid Willems Vaart and the Maas-Waal. The majority of this force, was made up of British and Canadian units from the 21st Army Group and its total strength was 9000 Sappers and 2277 (1250 RE /RCE and 1027 RASC/RCASC) vehicles.

On September 16th the SBF gathered at Bourg-Leopold, Belgium and were organized into columns; each column was controlled by one of the three AGRE (Army Group Royal Engineers) which was assigned a specific river to bridge in case the original bridge wasn't captured or had been destroyed. The Headquarters of the 11th AGRE was assigned the Maas River, the HQ of the 1st Canadian AGRE commanded both the Maas-Waal Canal and the Waal River and the 10th AGRE was responsible for the Neder Rijn River.

The general plan was that the AGRE and the administrative platoons of the Bridge Companies were to move forward to bridge the rivers. Each AGRE was to carry sufficient bridge equipment to bridge one of the rivers. The plan for bridging each river went as follows:

- for the Maas River; to immediately ferry tanks over on three Class 40 rafts. At the same time two bridges would be built. One was to be a floating Class 9 (for vehicles up to and including 9 tons, jeeps and most trucks) and the other was a Class 40 Bailey Bridge supported by pontoons (Bailey Pontoon Bridge).

Seven days later, another Class 40 Bailey Bridge would be built, but would be supported by barges instead of pontoons (Bailey Barge Bridge). The bridging column consisted of 878 vehicles;

- for the Maas-Waal; initially a Class 40 Bailey Pontoon Bridge would be built and quickly followed by another bridge of the same type; the bridging column consisting of 483 vehicles;

- for the Waal River; initially nine Class 40 rafts would operate until a Class 40 Bailey Pontoon Bridge could be built; the bridging column consisted of 380 vehicles;

- for the Neder-Rijn; immediately span the river with a Class 9 Bridge followed by a Class 40 Bailey Pontoon Bridge and a Class 40 Bailey Barge Bridge; the bridging column consisted of 536 vehicles.

Due to the single highway that all elements of the ground operation were forced to travel on, XXX Corps would control all movement on the route. The bridging columns would each have code names and convoy serial numbers and would be called forward as needed. A series of code words were set up to indicate the situation that the lead formation had encountered and what columns were required. (See Appendix #9 for a detailed list.) Each bridge company was made up of a headquarters, 10 platoons of trucks, a workshop and its own engineer platoon. In total, each company was over 450 vehicles and 700 men. A bridge dump, which contained all the bridging material, was set up just outside of Bourg-Leopold and was supervised by an engineer platoon from each of the bridge companies involved. The British 24th Transport Column (Bridging) RASC from the 2nd Army supplied the Bridge Companies. In September 1944, the unit had under its command:

85th Canadian Bridge Coy., RCASC
86th Canadian Bridge Coy., RCASC (not used in Op. M/G)
106th Bridge Coy., RASC
128th Bridge Coy., RASC
147th Bridge Coy., RASC
551st General Transport Company, RASC

Besides the two Canadian bridge companies, which were part of the 24th Transport Column, there were other Canadian formations which participated in Market Garden. The 1st Canadian Army Group Royal Engineers (AGRE), consisting of the ICAT, RCE and IICAT, RCE were attached to the SBF, and this was to include the 23rd Field Company, RCE. These Troops were used differently from the formation engineer units found in the divisions or at the Corps level and hence had different training and assignments; usually, this had to do with crossing major water obstacles. The only significant group of Canadians to be involved in the ground operations were the CANLOAN (junior Canadian Officers loaned to Britain to fill up the shortage in the British Army) officers spread throughout the British Army. These were officers, primarily lieutenants, who had volunteered in 1944 to serve in British units which had suffered severe casualties among their own junior officers. The surplus of Canadian officers was due to the disbanding of two territorial defense divisions in Canada. One of these officers was the future historian, Leo Heaps, who served with the British 1st Airborne throughout Operation Market Garden.

As of September 15th 1944, the Canadian engineer contribution to the SBF consisted of:

1st Canadian Army Group Royal Engineers
(Col. C.J. Bermingham)

1st Canadian Army Troops, RCE (Lt. Col. N.I. Byrn)
5th Field Company, RCE
20th Field Company, RCE
23rd Field Company, RCE
10th Field Park Company, RCE
3rd E + M Platoon (attached to 10th Field Park, RCE)

2nd Canadian Army Troops, RCE (Lt. Col. A.J. Kerry)
32nd Field Company, RCE
33rd Field Company, RCE
34th Field Company, RCE
11th Field Park Company, RCE

The IICAT, RCE was assigned the crossings up to and including the Waal River at Nijmegen while the ICAT, RCE had only to be concerned with the Neder Rijn at Arnhem. The reason why these units drew these assignments was because of their special training and experience in crossing broad and difficult waters. This fact shouldn't be taken lightly because they must have been very specialized and/or efficient to warrant a transfer from the Canadian 1st Army to the British 2nd Army for this operation, and be given the toughest of all the engineering assignments. There were other engineer units in the area, but it was the men of 1st Canadian AGRE who were given this assignment. Maybe it was because they had received praise from every unit CO that had used their services. At that time, the 23rd Field Company, RCE in particular had a reputation for being a 'hot' unit that could get the job done. It seems that their previous operations of effectively ferrying men and machines across the Seine had been noticed.

It was planned that by the time XXX Corps reached and crossed the Waal, the Guards Armoured Division would relinquish its lead position in the ground offensive to the 43rd Wessex Division, which would continue the advance to Arnhem and into Germany. From the start, it was expected that the engineers of ICAT were going to be under the command of the 43rd Wessex Division's CRE (Commander Royal Engineers), Lieutenant-Colonel Henniker, since they were tasked with bridging the Lower Rhine even though they were attached to the headquarters of the 10th AGRE.

In the general spirit of optimism that encompassed the operation, the engineers of ICAT believed that if they were to be committed at all, then it was to assist the advance of XXX Corps, whether by a river crossing or by bridging a river destroyed by the retreating enemy. The emphasis was to keep the fighting units of the Corps pushing ahead until all the airborne troops were relieved. There was little thought to the possibility that they would be employed to evacuate troops from an over-extended position. Since it was crucial that XXX Corps quickly link-up with all the airborne elements, the SBF was to keep itself ready to move at a moment's notice.

Operation Market Garden: The Attack

Day 1: Sunday, 17 September 1944
Weather: clear and cold

The start of the operation for the 23rd Field Company, RCE, the rest of ICAT and its supporting units typified what was to come for the next few days; which was very little. As fighting units struggled to obtain objectives, the engineers got into position and awaited orders. At 1040 hours the 23rd Field Company, RCE drove to a wooded area near Hechtel, approximately 12 km from the operation's start line.

In this quiet spot, free from any recently liberated locals bearing gifts, they were allowed to catch up on their sleep. Late in the afternoon, the sky filled with transport planes, gliders, tugs and their fighter escorts. These would have been the planes on the southern route transporting the first wave of the U.S. 101st Airborne Division. No one could doubt that something on a grand scale was happening. The massive artillery barrage laid down by XXX Corps at 1415 hours accentuated this fact. Shortly after, the Guards Armoured Division started their attack and the rush to join up with the Airborne units was on.

It was a beautiful day and as the men of the 23rd were enjoying the rest and wondering if their talents would be needed, a battalion of British paratroopers, under the command of Colonel John Frost, had captured the north end of the road bridge at Arnhem. This bridge was one of their three objectives. The other two were the railway bridge and the pontoon bridge; all three spanned the Neder Rijn. Unfortunately, the Germans blew up the railway bridge on the first day and the middle part of the platoon bridge was found to be missing. With two of the three water crossings over the Lower Rhine gone, the paratroopers needed to hold onto the road bridge. Unbeknownst to the 23rd and the generals, these events made the odds rise considerably that the 23rd and their Storm boats were going to be needed.

Day 2: Monday, 18 September 1944
Weather: fair and warm

For this day, the 23rd's War Diary stated: *"The unit again rested today, waiting for orders from 30 Br. Corps. It is expected that the coy will take part in the assault crossing of the NEDER RIJN in HOLLAND."* [20] The last sentence was included in the diary because that is what the 'insurance plan' had assigned to them, and that is what Major Tucker wanted to be prepared for. However, at this time, hardly anyone thought that an evacuation would be needed. Like the general mood of the Allied Forces in early September 1944, they thought only of the idea of advancing and ending the war. Nothing else was realistically entertained. Retreat was what the Germans were doing.

A rumour circulated amongst the men that Airborne troops had landed in The Netherlands and had captured the bridges over the Maas, Waal and Neder Rijn. This was good news if it was true. The bad news, unknown to them, was that heavy fighting had broken out around the Arnhem bridge. The mixed force with Colonel Frost's 2nd Battalion, The Parachute Regiment as its nucleus, was surrounded and the rest of the division was having a difficult time getting to them. South of Arnhem, the U.S. 82nd and 101st Airborne Divisions were more successful with their assigned objectives. However, the 101st Airborne Division had been unable to prevent the bridge at Son, across the Wilhelmina Canal, from being blown up and the 82nd Airborne Division had failed to capture either the road or rail bridges at Nijmegen. Unfortunately, both of these events would prove to have grave consequences for the British at Arnhem.

Day 3: Tuesday, 19 September 1944
Weather: fair and cool

On Tuesday the 23rd's War Diary stated: *"Again today the unit merely stood by awaiting orders. 1 and 2 Cdn A Tps. Engrs. are the only Cdn Troops in this area, and are under 1 and 10 CAGRE's respectively; but both are under 30 British Corps for the operation. Airborne Divs have been dropped on the 3 crossings of the RHINE Estuary in Northern Holland, and the amount of bridging that will be required on the 3 major obstacles will depend on the success of these divs."* [21]

It is clear from this that pieces of information were starting to filter back to the officers of the unit and they were forming a picture of what was going on. However, the men of the 23rd were still pretty much in the dark as to how critical the events at some of the objectives had become. According to Sapper Clayton Moss, *"The Maple Leaf paper knew more of what was going on at the front than we did. We had no idea what was going on. We just kept busy [with routine maintenance]. There was always something to do."* [22]

At Son, the engineers of the Guards Armoured Division had been busy. The 14th Field Company, RE had worked throughout the night erecting a 110' long Bailey bridge to span the Wilhelmina Canal; allowing XXX Corps to continue towards its objective of crossing the Lower Rhine. At 06:15 in the morning, the bridge was completed, allowing the Grenadier Guards Group to take over the vanguard from the Irish Guards Group, leading the way up to what would soon be known as *Hell's Highway*. Due to a number of delays the ground element was 36 hours behind schedule. Meanwhile at Arnhem, the 1st Airborne Division's final attempt to break through to the road bridge had failed; leaving Colonel Frost's force isolated and desperately holding only the north end of the bridge. Without the additional firepower of the remainder of the division, there was little hope that both ends of the bridge could be secured. Since it was becoming ever more apparent that the entire 1st Airborne Division would be trapped on the north side of the Lower Rhine, it was assured that the talents of the 23rd Field Company, RCE would be needed in some capacity.

Day 4: Wednesday, 20 September 1944
Weather: fair and cool

The minimal entry for Wednesday September 20th reflects only what was happening elsewhere; indicating that the 23rd was still standing by waiting for orders. The War Diary read:

"Still no orders to move, the leading Div of 30 Br Corps (the

Guards Armoured) has linked up with the airborne tps [troops] as far on as the second obstacle on the Rhine Estuary (the WAAL) at NIJMEGEN." [23]

The 85th Bridge Company, RCASC War Diary states for this day: *"The morale is not so good, no mail and this waiting is getting on everybody's nerves."* [24]

The same problems were evident at the 23rd's camp. Sapper Clayton Moss commented: *"During this time the Major was always making speeches in order to keep up our morale."* [25]

By now, all organized resistance at the Arnhem bridge had been overcome and the last crossing of the Neder Rijn was in enemy hands. Unfortunately, to the west of the bridge the remainder of the British 1st Airborne Division was trapped on the north side of the river. The only good news was that the Nijmegen road and railway bridges had finally been captured and the Allied units were moving into the area they referred to as 'The Island', but the Dutch called the Betuwe region. 'The Island' was the name given to the land bounded by the Lower Rhine in the north and the Waal in the south. To the east it ended at the Rhine River and in the west ended where the flat boggy land along the Lower Rhine and Waal almost joined together. It was almost literally an island in the middle of a country.

To capture the bridges at Nijmegen the 3rd Battalion of the 504th Parachute Infantry Regiment (of the U.S. 82nd Airborne Division) used 26 Assault boats provided to them by the Guards Armored Division's engineers. These boats were 19'-0" long with a flat plywood bottom and canvas sides 30 inches high, which were held up by wooden struts. To move across the river they were powered by the engineers of the 82nd Airborne Division with paddles. These overloaded and flimsy boats were pushed out into a fast moving river, during daylight and in full view of the enemy. Only thirteen boats returned to the south bank after the initial assault; 160 out of 260 men in the first wave were casualties.

This amphibious assault would have been an ideal use of Storm boats. With a much faster crossing time, the casualties would have been significantly fewer. Unfortunately, the men with the right equipment and the experience using it were at the wrong end of a long and congested corridor. As part of Market Garden's "insurance policy," IICAT, RCE of the Special Bridging Force was slated for an assault crossing of the Waal River. Their senior officers and reconnaissance parties were already in Nijmegen, but their companies were still at the start line.

Traffic problems alone don't explain the chaos of the engineers' role during Operation Market Garden. It was as if those in charge had forgotten the role that the SBF had been assembled for: to insure success crossing all river obstacles. Instead of units from the SBF, the Guards Armoured Division engineers supplied the boats for the Waal crossing. Still, it seems clear that the plan for the SBF never had the chance to be properly executed because General Gavin (CO of the U.S. 82nd Airborne Division) didn't know - or didn't remember the SBF when he asked if XXX Corps had any boats. General Horrocks (CO of XXX Corps) should have known*. Instead, Brigadier C.P. Jones, the CRE of the Guards Armoured Division was asked by XXX Corps if he had any assault boats at hand. He replied that he had 32 of them ready. Nowhere did he even mention the large engineer force waiting in the south.

The IICAT, RCE should have ferried the U.S. paratroopers** across the Waal River in their Storm boats. To be in position to do this, they should have been near the head of the column when XXX Corps reached Nijmegen. It's unlikely that the generals didn't know long before they got there that those bridges were still in the enemy's hands. For whatever reason, the Special Bridging Force wasn't called on. So far the SBF wasn't being used and was just sitting idly by in and around Bourg-Leopold.

With the Germans regaining control of the Arnhem bridge, it was now clear that the Special Bridging Force's insurance policy needed to be called upon. If the generals realized this the only questions should have been exactly how and where they would be used. The officers of the 23rd Field Company, RCE started to

---

* = he should have had an engineer officer with him as part of his small TAC as I stated in detail in, 'Bridging the Club Route'.

** = or the 43rd Wessex Division as originally slated to make the crossing.

think that they would be used in the assault role because this had been the role foreseen for them. They were convinced of this when they were ordered forward to Nijmegen the next day. Finally, the generals were getting something right.

Top Left: Corporal Robinson and L/Cpl. Riehl. (Russ Kennedy)
Top Right: Harold Barr. (Ryan Barr)
Above: taken from the Bedford Town Bridge, October 1943. On the back of the photos states: Lt. Millworth being thrown in after winning a rowing race.' It was probably Lt. Millward. (Ryan Barr)

Photos of the headquarters officers taken in October 1944.

Left: Bob Tate wrote on the back of his photograph: `Captain Don McIntyre, the 2 i/c of the 23rd. A good headquarters officer'. He was from Queens and was wounded in November during Operation Pegasus II. He happily recovered in a U.S. hospital. (Russ Kennedy)

Right: Lt. Charlie Aspler, a trained architect from Montreal who stared out as the company's recce officer, but became the HQ platoon officer in July. (Russ Kennedy)

Above: CSM Humphreys getting a ride in a Storm boat.

Right: Lt. Blair with CSM Humphreys after Operation Berlin. Lt. Blair joined the company after Operation Berlin.

Above: Lieutenant John Cronyn, in charge of 1st platoon. He was the nephew of the actors Hume Cronyn and Jessica Tandy.

On The Move Finally!

Day 5: Thursday, 21 September 1944
Weather: fair and warm

At 0845 an `O' Group (orders group) was held at CRASC, 24th Transport Column and orders were delivered. A similar meeting was held at 0915 at XXX Corps' CRE Headquarters. All orders were the same: it was time to move out. They were ordered forward to Nijmegen. At the time it was the furthest point north that XXX Corps had made contact with elements of the airborne forces.

The 85th Bridge Coy, RCASC held an `O' Group at 1000 hours and it was stated that only the Company Headquarters, `K' and `J' (Floating Bridge Equipment) platoons, `L' (Raft) platoon and one section of the workshop platoon were to be part of the column moving forward that day. The Column is to be known as BERTRAM serial numbers R724, R725 and R726. The balance of all three serials of BERTRAM Column was to be composed of various engineer companies and equipment including bulldozers. All vehicles were to be lined up in the field near present location at 1200 hours. Every vehicle in the column had BERTRAM and serial number stenciled in front and behind.

The 23rd War Diary states for this day: *"The O.C. and Lt. Kennedy left for a RV with CRE near Nijmegen on the Rhine Estuary at 0915 hrs. The unit moved off at 1015 hrs to be marshalled into a large bridging convoy between BOURG LEOPOLD and HECHTEL, at 1210 hrs the convoy moved off from HECHTEL with 23 Cdn Fd Coy leading, and with priority over everything on CLUB route as far north as GRAVE (on the MAAS RIVER IN HOLLAND). From Grave the convoy was met and guided into harbour area just south of NIJMEGEN at MR 700600 sheet 2A. The unit arrived in its area at approx 1700 hrs."* [26]

At 09:15 on the 21st a reconnaissance party consisting of Lieutenant Russ Kennedy, Sergeant Don Barnes and Sapper

Buck McKee were given passes for the "Arnhem Road" and then headed up the corridor. They were to meet with the CRE near Nijmegen and then scout an area for an assault crossing over the Neder Rijn. Traffic along the single road was heavy. Lt. Kennedy remembers that, *"Traffic control was just not good enough and the endless line of vehicles moved by fits and starts. I remember being ready to start a war of my own at the sight of two drivers calmly changing a tire on the road and holding up one complete lane."* [27]

What he didn't know at the time was that the main reason they were held up for three hours was because the Germans had cut the road at Uden. The threat to the road was a problem that the members of the U.S. 101st Airborne Division and tanks from XXX Corps had been constantly dealing with since the two formations had linked up. When that was cleared, the traffic resumed its northward journey. Lt. Kennedy continues: *"By noon I'd made just the 18 miles to Eindhoven and gratefully fell in with our main engineers' convoy which was coming through under an absolute priority clearance and a Military Police escort."* [28]

The rest of the 23rd Field Company, RCE left at 1210 hours with the Military Police escort that the lieutenant mentioned and had a much easier time of it. To demonstrate how long the column was the 23rd Field Company, RCE left at 1210 hours, the 20th Field Company, RCE left at 1230 hours and the BERTRAM Column at 1330 hours. Some 483 vehicles in total all travelled nose to tail up a narrow road. The men were thrilled to see that all other traffic on the road moved aside to make way for them, making them feel very important. The 85th Bridge Company, RCASC War Diary states: *"Convoy moves off at 1330 A. hrs and pass every convoy on the road, including infantry, airborne tps, tanks and complete divs which are also pushing forward. The route is lined with vehs and on some occasions are triple banking to all BERTRAM Br. Coln pass them. The coln has complete priority on the road. Airborne tps can be seen protecting the flanks from slit trenches dug along the verges of the highway. It is quite evident that a good deal of fighting took place. Vehicles are still burning as we pass though EINDHOVEN'.* [29]

At 1600 hours, the convoy was shelled just south of Uden. Sapper G.A. Topping of the 20ᵗʰ Field Company, RCE was badly wounded by shrapnel and was evacuated to an American Field Hospital. Three weeks later he was on his way to England to recover.

At the head of the convoy, the 23ʳᵈ Field Company, RCE was the first to arrive at its new location near Hatert, at approximately 1700 hours, along the Maas-Waal Canal. Lieutenant Kennedy remembers the welcoming committee: *"By late afternoon we had settled under the shadow of some trees on a road just south of Nijmegen. Fighter planes zoomed by and it was a bit of a shock to see the black crosses close up. At Caen we'd never seen a German fighter plane flying low except when the pilot was running for his life."* [30] The unit got what they wanted - they were in the game now.

With enemy planes above, the rest of the convoy dispersed to 60 yard intervals. Fortunately, soon Allied fighters arrived to shoot down three of them in what the 20ᵗʰ Field Company, RCE's War Diary describes as, *"a very lively dog fight."* Unfortunately, during this air battle they witnessed the shooting down of a Spitfire which came down near the Petrus Church in Hees (near Nijmegen). The pilot, Flying Officer John Robert Brody of 16 Squadron, and three civilians were killed in the crash. The entire convoy had settled into their new position at Hatert by 2300 hours and awaited further orders. Further down the column members of the 3rd Canadian E+M platoon witnessed a German FW 190 fighter plane shoot down two Dakota transport aircraft, causing the column to come to a halt.

Day 6: Friday, 22 September 1944
Weather: cloudy and cool

At 0850 hours 5 Troop, C Squadron, 2nd Household Cavalry Regiment, which was XXX Corps reconnaissance unit, under the command of Captain Wrottesly, made contact with the 1st Independent Polish Parachute Brigade at Driel. This was the first tenuous link between XXX Corps and the Allied airborne troops on the Neder Rijn.

On the morning of September 22nd, General Urquhart received a radio message from XXX Corps stating that the 43rd Division was moving with all possible speed to link up with the 1st Airborne Division at Oosterbeek. However, Urquhart felt compelled to risk the lives of two of his senior officers in a crossing of the Neder Rijn to have them personally inform both General Horrocks and General Browning, deputy commander of the 1st Allied Airborne Army, how desperate the situation was for his division. He sent his Chief of Staff, Lieutenant Colonel Charles Mackenzie to liaise with XXX Corps, and his Chief Engineer, Lieutenant Colonel Edward Myers to coordinate the river crossing that could save the division. The two crossed over in broad daylight in a two-man rubber dinghy, reaching the south shore at approximately 1300 hours. They encountered only very sporadic small arms fire during the crossing.

After contact had been made with XXX Corps by the Polish position at Driel, Lt-Colonel Mackenzie attempted to reach Nijmegen, but due to the lack of a secure route on the Island he was unable to meet Horrocks or Browning until the next day. Meanwhile, Lt-Colonel Myers remained to help organize a crossing of Polish reinforcements that night. This was to prove an ad hoc affair without the support of engineers from the ground element. The only boats available for the first crossing of the Neder Rijn were seven small inflatable rubber dinghies. Four had come from a stock held by the British 1st Airborne Division and the rest from what the Polish brigade had procured on their own initiative from sources in England. These yellow dinghies were originally designed for aircrews whose planes were forced down over the sea. The crossing began at 2300 hours with expectations that 200 men could be ferried to the north bank during the night. However, only approximately 50 Polish soldiers were able to reach the Oosterbeek perimeter in the five crossings before German machine gun fire put a halt to the operation. It was quite clear to everyone involved that a more concerted effort would need to be made to force a crossing of the Lower Rhine; it also gave a taste of the reaction they could expect from the Germans.

With the tenuous link made between the Polish brigade and XXX Corps, there was speculation within the 23rd that their talents might soon be put to use. In anticipation of a forthcoming operation Major Tucker had a recce party, under the command of Lt. Kennedy and consisting of Lt. Tate, Sgt. Barnes and Sapper McKee, attached to the 43rd Wessex Division to gather any information which would assist the company in successfully achieving its objectives on the Neder Rijn.

Day 7: Saturday, 23 September 1944
Weather: cloudy and cool

An `O' Group was held at 1130 hours with the Chief Royal Engineer (CRE), Lieutenant-Colonel Mark Henniker, of the 43rd Wessex Division. He assigned the following task to the Canadian engineers: the 23rd Field Company, RCE would man the Storm boats in an assault crossing while 20th Field Company, RCE constructed class 40 rafts. The 5th Field Company, RCE were to assist the 204th Field Company, RE to construct a class 9 Bridge. The 10th Field Park Company, RCE wasn't assigned a job, but was told that part of their unit may be called upon to do some engine maintenance and boat repairs. All were placed

Above: Lieutenant-Colonel Mark Henniker, the CRE of the 43rd Wessex Division's and the architect of Operation Berlin. He was the original CRE of the British 1st Airborne Division.

under the command of the 43rd Wessex Division and stood by on 2 hours notice all day. British sappers of the 3rd Platoon of the 204th Field Company, RE ferried the Polish troops across the river in collapsible canvas Assault boats. The Polish troops were to strengthen the by now fully besieged British 1st Airborne Division. Lt. Kennedy accompanied the British Sappers to look for a suitable site to launch the Storm boats, as well as obtain all possible information on the disposition of both friendly and enemy forces in the area in which the 23rd Field Company, RCE was expected to operate.

Support for the latest Polish attempt to cross the Neder Rijn was possible because the 130th Brigade of the 43rd Wessex Division had linked up with the Poles at Driel in the afternoon by using side roads, which bypassed the German stronghold at Elst. The Polish brigade was supplied with 14 of the Assault boats that had survived the river crossing at Nijmegen. Although these boats were a vast improvement on the sad flotilla that had attempted to ferry them across the previous night, the crossing was still plagued with problems. The boats were not delivered until after midnight, which cost them precious hours of darkness to hide their latest attempt from German eyes. The support furnished by the single platoon of engineers proved to be inadequate as the Polish paratroopers were forced to paddle many of the boats through the strong current. This was a skill that they had never practiced and one which did not come naturally to them. The result was that only approximately 200 men were able to reach the north bank of the Rhine.

Russ Kennedy said of this night operation: *"At night we and the boats* (of the 204th Field Company, R.E.) *got together with the Poles and moved up towards the river. At one point we were moving along the railway embankment when the Germans decided to shell it with 88s. The Poles were definitely in bad humour. They had been kept sitting, waiting for days in England, dropped practically down the muzzles of a lot of anti-aircraft guns and now they couldn't get to the war, it was not time to be stumbling about if one didn't speak Polish. The operation was not very successful. Some 250 Poles plus some ammunition were put across, but I did-*

n't learn much.''' [31]

The engineers did succeed in moving the bulk of the 3rd Battalion, the anti-tank squadron and part of the headquarters company across the river. This addition of men, while welcomed, did no more than reinforce the faltering perimeter around Oosterbeek and certainly did not alleviate the threat of capitulation by the British forces north of the Neder Rijn.

However, others were able to learn valuable lessons from the night's fiasco. If there was to be any hope of moving large numbers of troops across the Rhine, in whatever direction, either more engineers would be needed to navigate the Assault boats through the strong currents or a different type of boat, one which provided its own power, would be needed.

At this point, with everyone but them fighting around and even above them, Major Tucker and his men were wondering why they weren't being used. The unit history asks: *"Why won't they let us play?"'* [32]

Also, it should be noted that at this time the Richard Column was working their way up the CLUB route. This was a very optimistic plan since the unit was appointed for bridging the Ijessel river. This meant that the generals had no idea how bad things were going for the British 1st Airborne Division in Oosterbeek and that they expected that a bridgehead over the Neder Rijn could be accomplished without detracting from the momentum of the advance. They would soon find out how badly they had misjudged events.

Day 8: Sunday, 24 September 1944
Weather: cloudy and cool

At last, the 23rd Field Company, RCE got word that they were going to be used and a reorganization of vehicle loads was ordered for the BERTRAM Column, Detail No 4 consisting of 18 trucks carrying Storm boats and Evinrude engines. The plan was that 10 of the Storm boats would be loaded tactically so they could be assembled with minimal hassle. For each truck there would be 1 boat and 1 engine. The rest of the column was organized with five trucks carrying 15 boats while the remaining three trucks carried 18 engines. This meant that in total the column was transporting 25 boats and 28 engines, 10 of which could be rapidly engaged. Due to this new arrangement, the remaining 11 boats and 8 engines were left behind because of a lack of transport. This was not the ideal situation, but it was thought that it was the best under the uncertain circumstances ahead.

The 23rd War Diary entry for the 24th: *"The unit received movement orders during the morning and moved off northwards in convoy, but got only as far as NIJMEGEN. The move was cancelled at approx 1300 hrs by CRE 43 and the Coy returned to its former area just south of NIJMEGEN. Lt. Kennedy, Sgt. Barnes and Spr. McKee returned from their recce with 260* (sic) *Fd. Coy and reported that several hundred Polish Airborne tps crossed the river to the aid of the surviving elements of their Div on the bridgehead on 24 Sep by night. Enemy mortar fire was brought down on the assault boats engaged in the crossings."* [33]

On this day, the 23rd Field Company, RCE marshaled with the Storm boat lorries on a road leading into Nijmegen. The 20th Field company, RCE was lined up behind them with their Assault rafts. Here they waited and waited until at last their movement order came. They joined Detail No. 6 and got a few miles down the road before the order was cancelled.

The war diary of `J' Platoon of 85th Bridge Coy. RCASC states why the operation was cancelled: *"The town of "Elst" was an enemy strong point from which he laid a deadly mortar, 88 and machine gun fire on anything that was moving on the roads. The column couldn't make the grade without suffering heavy casualties in both men and equipment, so it was decided to turn around and head back to the bivouac area."* [34]

All 483 vehicles returned to the bivouac area. Lieutenant Kennedy and his recce party had managed to rejoin them as they were marshaled, finding them to be a disappointed group. Almost all of the men in the column tried to get a good night's sleep in expectation of getting very little in the immediate future. However, twenty-five year old Sapper Clayton Moss spent most of the night talking to his tent mate, Sapper David Lloyd George Hope from New Brunswick. *"Oh, what we didn't talk about,"*

Clayton said. *"Neither one of us wanted to sleep that night. We knew that something big was up because Major Tucker was giving speeches to men to keep up morale. We didn't know what was going on. You just did what you were told to. And the Major's speeches were more and more frequent So something big was coming."* [35]

At the headquarters of XXX Corps, Lt General Horrocks ordered another attempt at crossing the Neder Rijn, opposite the British 1st Airborne Division's perimeter at Oosterbeek, for the night of the 24th/25th. This was to be undertaken by the 4th Battalion of the Dorsetshire Regiment and the remainder of the 1st Independent Polish Parachute Brigade. The objective was to reinforce the base of the Oosterbeek perimeter on the only high ground in the area that overlooks the river, the Westerbouwing Heights. This geographic feature rises 30m above the surrounding land. If this was successful, on the next night, 25/26 September, the rest of the 43rd Wessex Division would cross further to the west, establishing bridges across the Neder Rijn. From its bridgehead on the north bank the 43rd Division was to carry out a flanking attack on the rear of the von Tettau Division, to relieve the pressure on the remnants of the besieged airborne forces. There are conflicting accounts for the rationale behind Horrocks' orders. Brigadier Essame, the 43rd Wessex Division's historian and commander of its 214th Infantry Brigade understood that the 4th Dorsets were to cross only to secure a strong bridgehead on the north bank for the inevitable withdrawal. If this was the case then the decision to abandon all positions north of the Lower Rhine had already been made.

Before these orders could be implemented Lt General Horrocks attended a conference at Sint-Odenerode. This conference included Lt. General Sir Miles Dempsey, commander of 2nd British Army and Lt General F.A.M. Browning of the 1st Airborne Corps. That afternoon Horrocks outlined his plan to cross the Neder Rijn and relieve the 1st Airborne Division. However, Browning felt that this effort would be too late to save the 1st Airborne Division and advocated for a total withdrawal. Again, there are discrepancies over what was finally agreed upon at the conference. In Horrock's memoir, *Corps Commander*, approval was granted to the plan by Dempsey, but with the proviso that if the initial crossing was not successful then the forces on the north bank would be evacuated. This lends credence to the argument that parts of the British 2nd Army's command structure still did not fully comprehend how desperate the situation was for the British 1st Airborne Division or how strong their foe had become as they still felt there was a way to salvage the position north of the Neder Rijn. Dempsey, in other accounts, after conferring with Montgomery had already decided on withdrawal and rejected a final attempt to reinforce what he viewed as a lost cause.

The crossing of the Dorsets, under the command of Lt. Colonel Gerald Tilly, over the Neder Rijn on the night of 24/25 September was a series of disasters. The original plan called for two field companies of the 43rd Wessex Division's engineers, the 204th and the 553rd Field Companies, RE, to ferry both the Dorsets and the 1st Battalion Polish Parachute Brigade across the river in canvas Assault boats, although only the Dorsets eventually crossed. However, a lesson from the previous night's attempt to cross the river had been learned, and two full companies of engineers were assigned to navigate the boats, rather than just one platoon. This would be necessary if over a battalion of men were to cross in a single night. Setbacks to the operation began to occur that afternoon as the convoy of five trucks carrying the Assault boats was delayed when the Germans were able to cut one of the routes XXX Corps was using for its advance. This postponed the planned 2230 hours start time for the operation indefinitely, and reduced the hours of darkness available to ferry across the maximum number of troops. By the time the convoy reached the south bank of the river it consisted of only one truck carrying a total of nine boats, minus paddles. The other trucks of the convoy had been held up along the route by either the darkness or the rain as they were forced to travel after dark. Two of the vehicles made a wrong turn near their final destination and drove into enemy positions at Elst. The last two trucks were unable to negotiate the slippery roads in the dark and bogged down in the fields of the Island after sliding off the roads. With only nine boats available for the operation, the Polish forces were told their part in the operation was cancelled and to hand over the three assault boats they still possessed from the previous night's operation. The Polish craft came with paddles, which the recently received boats did not, compelling both the engineers and the infantry to use rifles to propel their boats across the river.

By the time the boats were in position on the south bank and the Dorsets were ready to embark, it was after 0200 hours, over three hours behind schedule. The noise of manhandling the Assault boats down to the mud flats along the river had alerted the Germans, who directed machine gun and mortar fire onto the embarkation site. This scene would play out again the next night for the 23rd Field Company, RCE. Some boats were hit by enemy fire while others were swept downstream by the strong current which Polish sappers had previously calculated flowing at 1.4 meters per second. Under covering fire provided by the 5th Dorsets and supporting artillery, two companies and some of the tactical HQ, totaling 315 officers and men, were able to cross the Lower Rhine before the operation was called off at 0430 hours. Along with the Assault boats three DUKWs (large amphibious trucks) loaded with medical supplies attempted to cross the river but became stuck in the muddy shores of the bank.

Very few of the Dorsets were able to successfully link up with the besieged Airborne in the Oosterbeek perimeter. Most had landed downstream in small groups in German held territory and were forced to surrender when they landed or later in the morning, after first light revealed their positions. Approximately 200 of the 315 men of the force were captured and unable to support the British 1st Airborne Division's defenses. The lack of success of the 4th Dorsets to secure a strong bridgehead on the north shore of the Neder Rijn removed any possibility that the British 1st Airborne Division's position could be held as a springboard for XXX Corps' crossing of the Neder Rijn. Consequently, the evacuation of the remaining Airborne troops would be postponed until the following night.

Operation Berlin

The Best Laid Plans

Day 9: Monday, 25 September 1944
Weather: clear and cold

In the morning, Major Tucker told his officers of an advance warning from Colonel Bermingham (OC of 1ˢᵗ CAGRE) that the Airborne troops might be pulled out of the perimeter across the Rhine. The area was to be somewhere east of the small town of Driel. This was top secret and they were to tell no one. Major Tucker attended an orders group at 43ʳᵈ Wessex Division Headquarters at 1000 hours. The decision had been passed down from General Horrocks that Operation Market Garden had failed and it was time to get the British 1ˢᵗ Airborne Division out. The code name for the withdrawal was Operation Berlin, suggested by General Urquhart, who hoped it would mislead the enemy of their true intentions of evacuation. Lieutenant-Colonel Henniker made it clear that the Storm boats were to be the primary means of evacuating the men from the north shore that night. It was hoped that the speed and power of the Storm boats would be able to overcome the swift currents and enemy fire encountered on the Neder Rijn during the two previous nights. However, Major Tucker was further informed that he could only rely on his own resources to deploy the boats to their launch sites. Shortly afterwards, Lieutenant Robert S. Tate joined the recce party along with Lieutenant Kennedy, Sgt. Barnes and Sapper McKee. They were to conduct a more thorough daylight search to find the launch site for that night's operation and to determine the disposition of both friendly and enemy units in the area. The addition of Lieutenant Tate to the recce party was, *"one of Mike's [Tucker's] better decisions"* in Kennedy's view. Sending the officers to reconnoiter the area would ensure that the information gathered would still reach the company, even if one of them was wounded. This was a very real possibility, as the recce party found out. *"We couldn't get past the infantry and down to the river because they didn't want someone out there drawing fire,"* a clear indication of how alert the enemy was to anyone reaching the British 1st Airborne Division from the south bank. So, together Kennedy and Tate examined as much of the waterfront as they could while trying to remain unobserved by the Germans on the northern bank.[36]

As the officer in charge of the recce, Lieutenant Kennedy described the area and the situation: *"A few hundred yards from the Rhine was the main or winter dyke, 18 or 20 feet high, with very steep sides. No cultivation of crops was allowed in front of it. Then perhaps 10 yards closer to the water was the summer dyke, 7 to 10 feet high. Finally the river bank itself was protected from erosion by groynes, narrow spurs built out every 100 or 150 yards or so, and faced with stone. On the north side one could see the low hills of Arnhem and Oosterbeek all quite unfriendly. The infantry of the 43rd, now holding posts at intervals back of the winter dyke, were anxious to keep us out of sight of the enemy and so we had to settle for occasional peeks over the crest. It was poor territory for a night action with Storm boats, but some sites were possible. The best seemed to be a fair-sized orchard just south of the winter dyke and located within the sector which had been indicated. It could be reached down a narrow muddy lane which was separated from the orchard by a ditch. If boats were to be taken in on trucks, the ditch would have to be bridged."'*[37]

The infantry he was referring to were the 5th Battalion of the Dorsets Regiment of the 130th Infantry Brigade, 43rd Wessex Division. They held the line from the blown railroad bridge along the river to the other side of Driel. When Lieutenant Kennedy's recce party returned, they were informed that the evacuation was to go ahead. The site Lieutenant Kennedy selected, although in his own mind was poor, had been judged acceptable for the operation.

At a second orders group, held at 1745 hours, Major Tucker

was informed of the timings for the night's events. The plan was for an artillery barrage to commence at 2100 hours, which was designed to keep the enemies' heads down, followed by the launching of the boats at 2130 hours. Two sites had been chosen on the south shore of the Neder Rijn to stage the evacuation. Two companies of engineers would silently paddle their canvas Assault boats across first, the 553rd Field Company, RE at the Driel Ferry site and the 260th Field Company, RE at the site opposite of the Oosterbeek church. Each site was to be reinforced by a RCE company equipped with Storm boats. The 20th Field Company, RCE would assist the 553rd at the ferry site and the 23rd would support the 260th.

Major Tucker thought that his unit wasn't being used to the full extent. He claimed that, *"We could have ferried reinforcements into Arnhem, instead of bringing the survivors out, as we did."* [38] What he didn't realize was how precarious the situation for the British 1st Airborne Division had become, and that the decision to scrap the position north of the Neder Rijn had been made at the conference at Sint Oedenrode on the previous day.

Unfortunately, however, the Generals had spoken. Operation Market Garden was over and Operation Berlin was in place. The determining factor for this decision was the lack of supplies. XXX Corps' resources were stretched too thin to force more than a limited bridgehead north of the river. Pushing on all the way to the Zuider Zee and the Ijessel was out of the question. The land corridor that had been forced open by XXX Corps was under considerable pressure from the German forces, whose constant shelling had earned it the nickname 'Hell's Highway'. Only the previous afternoon, German troops had succeeded in temporarily cutting the highway at Koevering, just to the north of Sint Oedenrode. The struggle to maintain a secure artery had diverted much of XXX Corps' resources and made it extremely difficult to move supplies and specialty troops forward. This was to have an impact on the operation scheduled to take place this night.

According to the 43rd Wessex Division's War Diary, the plan was as follows:

1) A fire plan to keep the enemies' heads down. This also in-

cluded AA firing tracers to mark the flanks of the operation.

2) A feint attack by 129 Brigade on the left. This included all the preparations for an assault crossing. As it was in full view of the enemy, there is no doubt that it had a good effect.

3) Four field companies to do the actual ferrying on two sites - 553 Fd Coy and 20 Cdn Fd Coy on the same site as the 4 Dorset crossing the night before and 260 and 23 Fd Coys on the ferry site opposite 1 Airborne Div. At each site there were 16 Assault boats and 21 Storm boats. 20 and 23 Fd Coys are Canadian Fd Coys from 10 AGRE and being expert with stormboats they used them whereas 553 and 260 Fd Coys used assault boats.[39]

Several errors are easily spotted in this report. One is that the location for the 260th and 23rd site, which was further east, was directly opposite of the base of the Airborne perimeter. Another error was the number of Storm boats that were to take part in the operation; there were twenty-two in total as opposed to the twenty-one stated at each site. Such mistakes are common in these kinds of reports. The stresses of war and poor communication can overpower the attention to detail.

Lieutenant-Colonel Henniker, the chief Engineer of the 43rd Wessex Division, was in charge of the entire ferrying operation. He had already met with Lieutenant-Colonel Myers of the British 1st Airborne Division, who would control the northern bank. As previously mentioned, the Airborne officer had crossed the river on 22 September to explain to XXX Corps how critical the situation was for the British 1st Airborne Division. In the early hours of 25 September Lieutenant-Colonel Myers had re-crossed the river with the letter from Major General Thomas, commanding officer of the 43rd Wessex Division, informing General Urquhart of the order to withdraw from the north side of the Neder Rijn.

As an ironic twist of fate, the officer who was now responsible for the evacuation of the British 1st Airborne Division had been 'forced out' of the division a few months earlier because they thought that he wasn't qualified. This was common practice for a unit that considered itself to be elite. Many men were sent back to their old units if they did not display the attributes deemed necessary for such a unit. Now their fate was in the hands of someone who they thought wasn't up to the job. In his own words, Lieutenant-Colonel Henniker stated: *"We studied a great many possible and impossible operations, and I found myself gradually getting more and more out of step with those I was working with. Never in my career had I been a "Yes-man", but I was finding to my dismay that I was rapidly becoming a positive "No-man."* [40]

He started to feel that he was becoming a "bolshie" officer" (an expression from the Bolshevik Revolution meaning difficult or argumentative) and before he knew it, General Urquhart addressed him: *"I think that you've been too long in this Airborne business. You've been Airborne for nearly three years and it's time you had an inning with an Infantry Division in Normandy. I'll help you to get a decent appointment in 21 Army Group, but will you tell me which of these Sappers I've been offered in your place is the best one?"* [41] He was shown a list of names and without hesitation, he chose Lieutenant-Colonel Eddie Myers. He thought that he would be a perfect choice for the new CRE of the British 1st Airborne Division.

On the same day that the British 1st Airborne Division was committing itself north of the Neder Rijn the man, who nine days later would be in charge of coordinating its evacuation, took over as the new CRE of the 43rd Wessex Division. Lt-Colonel Henniker took over after the previous CRE had been wounded in action. Luckily, the division was a follow-up unit in this operation so he had four days before they were committed to action to get to know his new command. Still, it was not enough time to establish a good working relationship with his subordinates or the divisional staff.

To carry out this mission, the 23rd Field Company, RCE had to relocate onto the Island. The terrain was described by Major Tucker as, *"low and boggy and the roads on the route are narrow, slippery and are built up well above normal ordinary ground levels. All entrances to the fields are narrow and difficult to negoti-*

ate even in full light. Make a mistake while driving in this country and your vehicle winds up in a deep wide ditch." [42] The landscape was a daunting challenge for the drivers just to deliver the boats to the starting point.

The unit would be based at Valburg, approximately six kilometers south of the evacuation site, parking the vehicles on the firm surface of the railing yard. This move was accomplished while Lieutenants Kennedy and Tate were still on their recce mission. The Storm boats were to be parked on the tree-lined street which screened its presence from any German planes flying over. Also, it was decided that a minimal number of vehicles would move on to Valburg from their present location near Hatert. The rest of the company stayed behind under the command of a disappointed Captain McIntyre. Since the situation was constantly changing and anything might happen, Major Tucker thought it was best that a good officer was left behind. The possibility that they could be cut off from each other for a long period of time was great and Major Tucker needed to be assured that the remainder of the company was in competent hands. This decision was high praise for Captain McIntyre's leadership skills, although little consolation for a dedicated officer who wished to see action.

Only the working personnel of the company and just enough administrative personnel to attend to the unit's most urgent needs were packed into 3 jeeps, 2 scout cars, 2 kitchen trucks and 12 3-ton trucks. Lieutenant Kennedy's recce party left to make contact with the 130th Infantry Brigade, under the command of Brigadier B. Walton, to finalize the unloading and launching sites.

At 1400 hours trucks carrying the 20th Field Company, RCE, the Storm boat lorries and a 3 ton truck carrying the maintenance party from the 10th Field Park Company, RCE joined them. The men from the field park company would be divided into 2 sections, each led by a Lance Sergeant and consisting of 4 engine fitters and an electrician for minor repairs to the outboard motors and 2 carpenters for minor repairs to the Storm boats. (See Appendix #2 for complete listing of the men involved.)

The precariously slow drive to Valburg was done safely and there they dispersed their vehicles and boats according to plan. While the force was having their dinner, a squadron of German fighters flew over Valburg, but since the boats were hidden under the trees they weren't seen. Otherwise it would have been a disastrous night for the British 1st Airborne Division because it would have forewarned the Germans that a large-scale river crossing was imminent and the boats would have been the prime target for an air raid.

Lieutenant Cronyn remembers them being the new jets and not too impressed with them: *"They were obviously scraping the bottom of the barrel and were using these experimental aircraft more for show and for reconnaissance than anything else."* [43] The jets that he saw were Messerschmitt ME 262 aircraft from Kampfgeschwader 51, which had been enlisted to destroy the bridges at Nijmegen. The ME 262s, along with a variety of Luftwaffe bombers and dive-bombers, launched daily attacks on both the road and railway bridges from 25 to 29 September. They could have easily been redirected to an engineering column unfortunate enough to be detected in an exposed position.

As the 23rd waited for darkness, Lieutenant Bob Tate, who had participated in the daytime recce, left at 1845 hours with a section from 2nd Platoon in one truck to bridge the ditch into the orchard. One of the men that he brought along was Corporal Robinson. He was a quiet, thoughtful man who was just over 6 feet tall, from Tompkins, Saskatchewan. He was the son of a prairie blacksmith, and could make almost anything. Constructing the bridge was to be the first of many tasks that he would perform that night. This orchard was, of course, under full observation from the enemy on the Westerbouwing Heights. It was hoped that a lone truck wouldn't draw artillery fire that would be attracted by a convoy. Fortunately, the German preoccupation with reducing the Oosterbeek pocket ensured that the overcrowded truck was left alone. It arrived at the selected spot and the team started to work immediately to bridge the ditch between the muddy lane and the orchard. The bridge into the orchard was finished around 2000 hours.

Above: Three NCOs. George Robinson, George King and S. Strong.
(George and Ethel King)

Sapper Donald Somerville, another member of Tate's bridging party remembers: *"As we got closer to the river you could hear the heavy mortar and machine gun fire. When we arrived at our destination, we unloaded some of the ties and rails to put across the ditch or moat so the trucks could cross into the orchard, leading up to the first dike wall. The shelling got quite heavy a few times while working on the abutment for the bridge, a few of us jumped into the water."* [44]

Above: L to R: Sappers H.C. Martin, D. McDonald and J.W. Black. Black was the unit's only casualty on the move to the orchard. He took a piece of shrapnel in the arm, which only temporarily put him out of action. (Russ Kennedy)

Above: Donald Somerville. He pointed out to me that the location of the bridge
on the map in the first edition of The Storm Boat Kings wasn't exactly right
and we worked together to try to figure out exactly where it was located. I vis-
ited the site and showed him dozens of photos of the area when I got back. After
many discussions we have found the spot of the bridge. See the updated map on
page 74. (Donald Somerville)

To The Orchard and Into The Mud

Lieutenant Charley Aspler, an architect from Montreal, was put in charge of the men left behind in Valburg as the remainder of the company crammed into 3 jeeps, a scout car and 3 3-ton trucks. It was the minimal amount of vehicles necessary to carry all the men and equipment. This left Lieutenant Aspler in charge of a scout car, nine 3-ton trucks and two kitchen trucks. Sapper Clayton Moss said that he and others even had to ride in the Storm boats due to the lack of room in the personnel carriers. With them were the Roman Catholic Padre from ICAT, RCE, Captain Jean Mongeon, and half the maintenance party from the 10th Field Park Company, RCE. The maintenance party had left their carpenters behind since this was a night operation and they needed light for their work. The Protestant padre, Captain Brown, and the other half of the maintenance party were in the convoy for the 20th Field Company, RCE. Commenting on this the Major joked: *"Even from the start the two sections of the river was divided along religious grounds."* [45]

The convoy also included 17 trucks* carrying the Storm boats for both the 20th and the 23rd. Closer to the river this convoy would break off into two groups, each one going to their assigned field company. Russ Kennedy recalls the move: *"As it*

* = One of the 18 trucks had broken down and its three Storm boats were left behind.

Right and opposite page: the route that the company took to get from Nijmegen to Valburg and then to the Driel.

Route Card Nijmegen — Arnhem

Nijmegen R.R. Bridge 704632
① Turn left at first x—rds (708639)
② x—rds 676663
③ x—rds 677668, turn left
④ Rd. Junction 661674, turn right
⑤ Road junction 663679, turn left
⑥ Valburg x—rds 662700, turn right
　Intermediate harbour along this road
⑦ Road junction 691709, turn left
⑧ Road junction 680746
　x—rds 680754 DRIEL
　Marshalling harbour in this vicinity

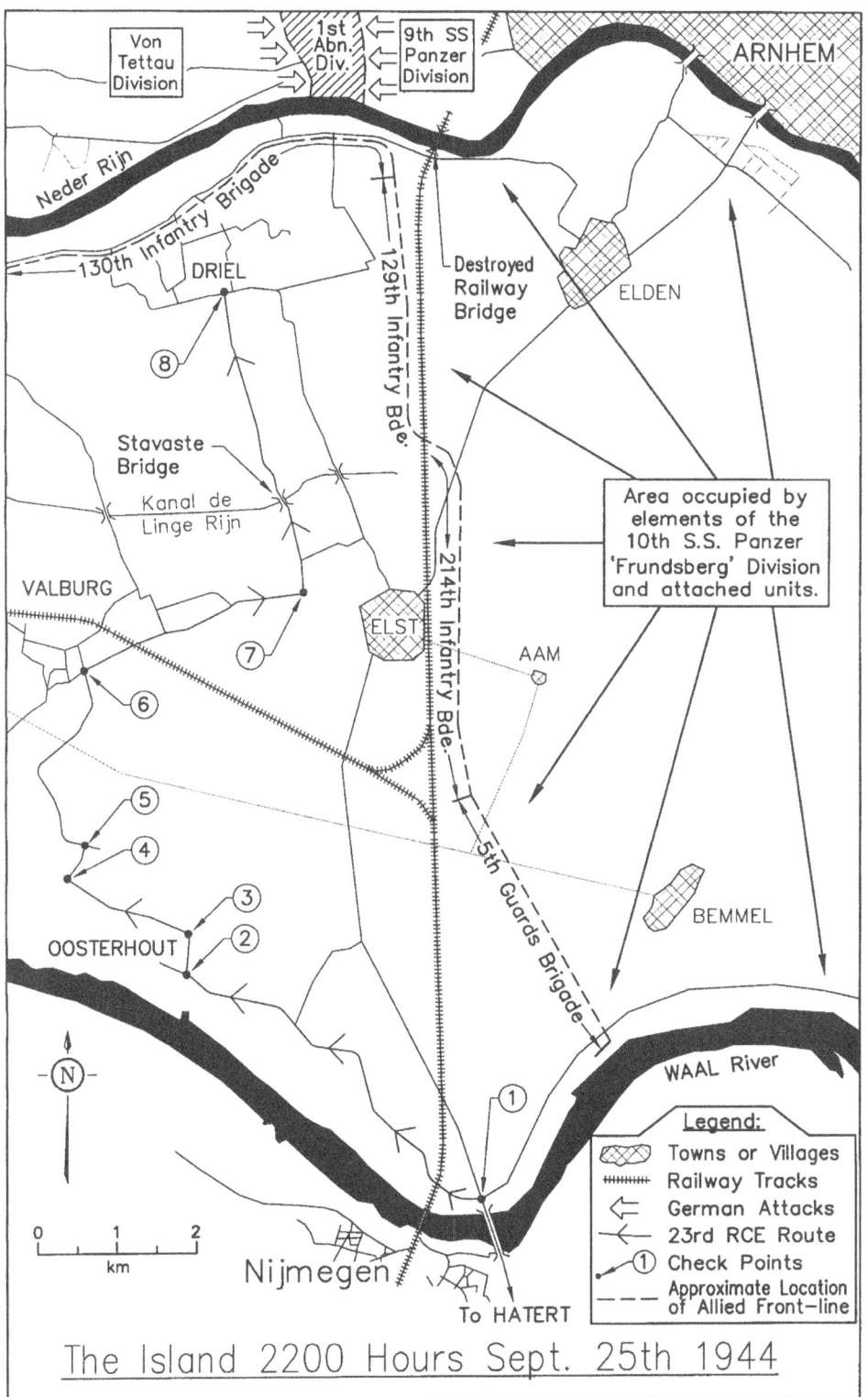

Von Tettau Division

1st Abn. Div.

9th SS Panzer Division

ARNHEM

Neder Rijn

130th Infantry Brigade

129th Infantry Bde.

DRIEL

⑧

Destroyed Railway Bridge

ELDEN

Stavaste Bridge

Kanal de Linge Rijn

214th Infantry Bde.

Area occupied by elements of the 10th S.S. Panzer 'Frundsberg' Division and attached units.

VALBURG

ELST

AAM

⑦

⑥

⑤

④

③

②

OOSTERHOUT

5th Guards Brigade

BEMMEL

-N-

WAAL River

①

Legend:

Towns or Villages

Railway Tracks

German Attacks

23rd RCE Route

① Check Points

Approximate Location of Allied Front-line

0   1   2
km

Nijmegen

To HATERT

The Island 2200 Hours Sept. 25th 1944

73

*got dark, we moved off with 24 vehicles, just enough to carry our
men and the 14 storm boats. The road was twisting, muddy and
slippery."* 46

It was 1915 hours when the convoy left Valburg. The most
likely division of the trucks would be that the 23rd Field Company, RCE had 5 lorries loaded tactically (1 boat, 1 engine each),
3 lorries with 3 boats each and 2 lorries carrying engines only.
While the 20th Field Company, RCE had 5 boats loaded tactically, one lorry with 3 boats and one truck carrying engines only.

The total number of Storm boats was twenty-two. Eight
boats were assigned to the 20th and the lion's share of boats was
allocated to the 23rd who were to setup directly opposite of what
was believed to be the middle of the 1st Airborne Division's position. Major Tucker had been told at Lieutenant-Colonel Henniker's orders group that the Oosterbeek Laag church was the cen-
ter of the Airborne's perimeter. He was also told that they were
on their own and not to expect any assistance from XXX Corps,
who were struggling to hold open the corridor.

The 20th Field Company, RCE added to the convoy as they
headed north towards Driel. Prior to their journey, Military
Police were placed at each crossroad to prevent any vehicles
going astray on the twisting, muddy and very slippery roads, as
had happened the previous night. Two Assault boat trucks
assigned to support the 204th Field Company, RE had missed a
turn and drove straight into the German lines where they were
shot-up and captured. *"For me it was the most worrisome part of
the job,"* Lt. Kennedy remembered. *"We couldn't use the route we
had taken earlier in the day and one wrong turn would have
meant hours of delay and disaster for the Airborne still alive and
waiting for us."* 47 Fortunately, the Military Police kept everyone
on the right road despite the conditions of the roads. It was completely dark by the time they reached the Stavaste Bridge and as
they got closer to within range the enemy sent up flares and then
started shelling the road. Lieutenant John Cronyn comments:
*"German 88s opened up on us and were cracking overhead much
too close for comfort."* 48 Luckily, only one member of the unit was
wounded during this precarious drive, when shrapnel hit the

elbow of Sapper Black. The piece of flying metal didn't penetrate the flesh or break the bone and Sapper Black's arm was only temporarily paralyzed.

The convoy reached the bridge built by Lieutenant Tate and his men leading into the Orchard at 2010 hours. First over were the jeeps and the Scout car. Then the problems started to occur. When the first lorry was about to cross the narrow bridge its front wheels slipped off the road and became stuck. According to Sapper Donald Somerville, *"The first truck did not turn sharp enough and the front wheel dropped off the side of the bridge. There was a tank near by, so we asked if they would fire a few round from the machine gun to kill the noise of the truck engine, as it tried to back up."* [49] *

At this point several members of the company reported that they had seen trucks carrying men from the 23rd mistakenly follow the Storm boat trucks assigned to the 20th Field Company.

Above: the road up to the winter dyke. The apple orchard where the 23rd Field Coy. R..C.E. unloaded their Storm boats is on the right.

* = at the book launch at Russ Kennedy's family cottage, Russ and Donald both remembered turning opposite ways into the orchard. As I listened to them I came to the conclusion that the main party and Lt. Tate's party took 2 different routes.

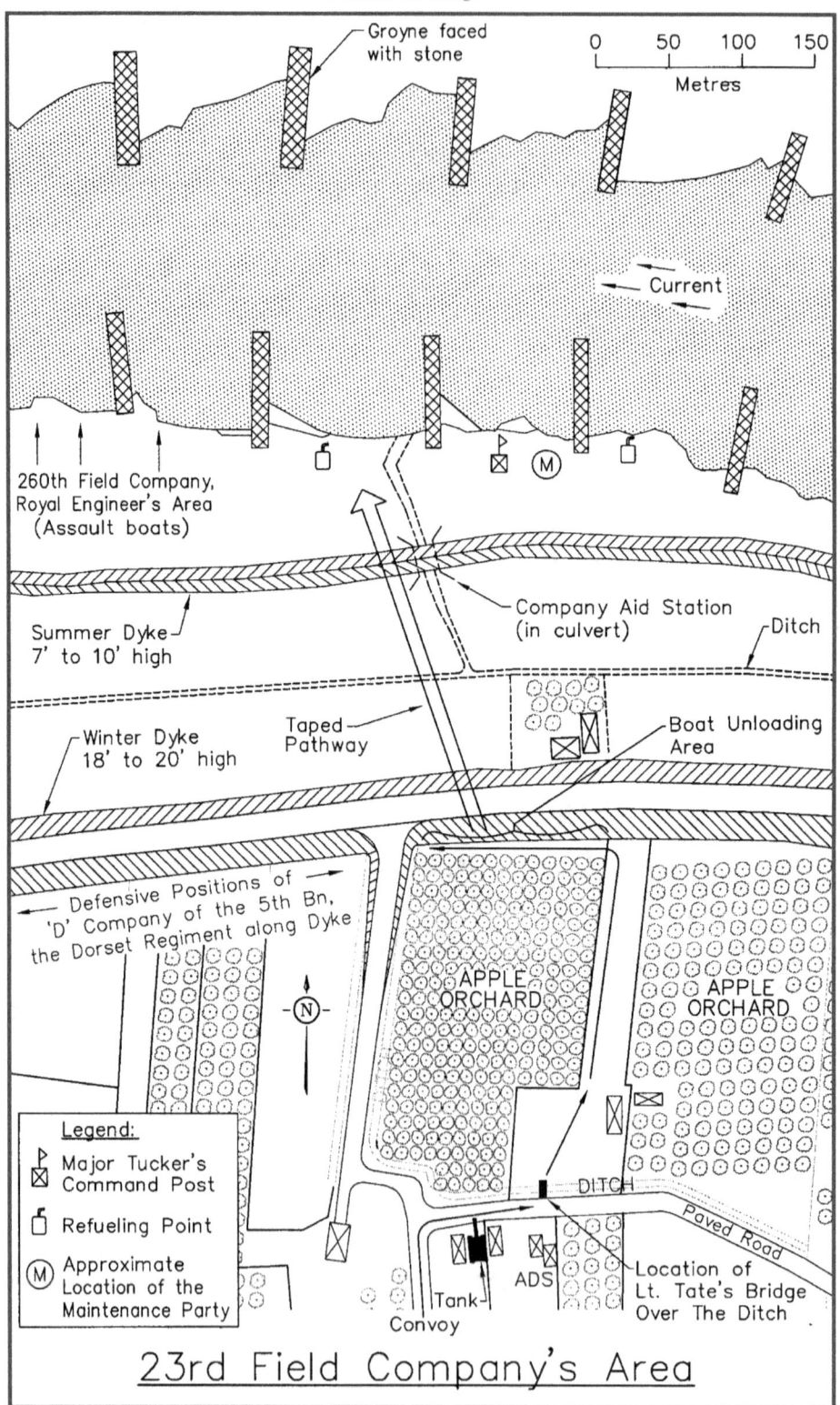

Groyne faced
with stone

0   50   100   150
Metres

← Current →

260th Field Company,
Royal Engineer's Area
(Assault boats)

Company Aid Station
(in culvert)

Ditch

Summer Dyke
7' to 10' high

Winter Dyke
18' to 20' high

Taped
Pathway

Boat Unloading
Area

Defensive Positions of
'D' Company of the 5th Bn,
the Dorset Regiment along Dyke

APPLE
ORCHARD

APPLE
ORCHARD

Legend:

▷ Major Tucker's
⊠ Command Post

⌂ Refueling Point

Ⓜ Approximate
Location of the
Maintenance Party

DITCH

Paved Road

Location of
Lt. Tate's Bridge
Over The Ditch

Tank
Convoy

ADS

23rd Field Company's Area

76

Above: a December 1944 aerial shot of the 23rd Field Company's area of operation on the night of September 25/26 1944. The apple orchard is in the middle of
the picture.

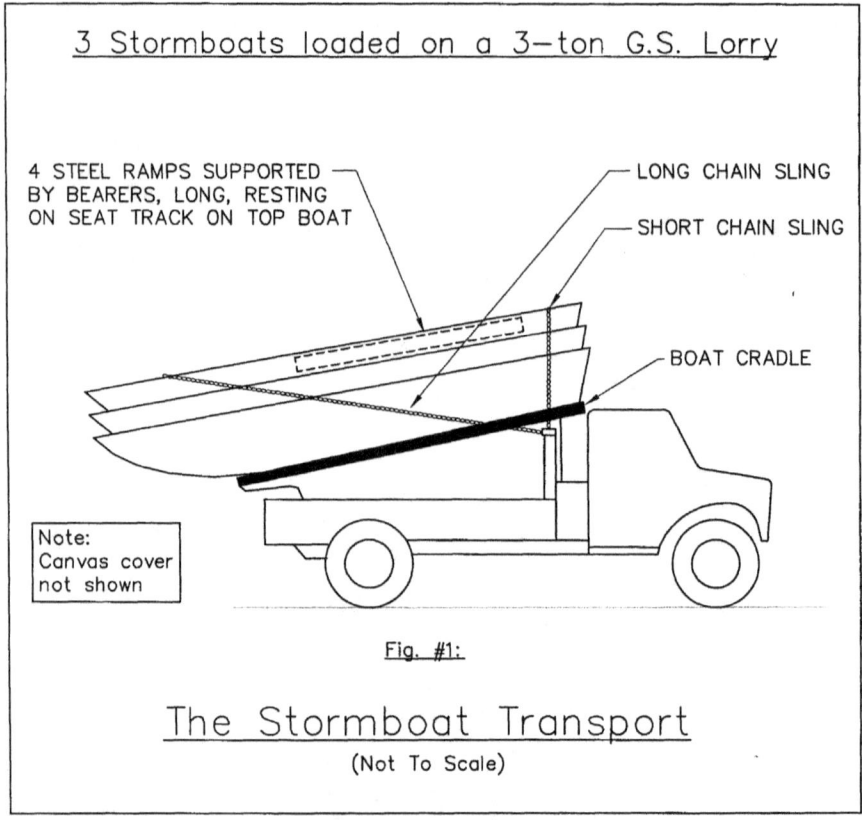

3 Stormboats loaded on a 3-ton G.S. Lorry

4 STEEL RAMPS SUPPORTED
BY BEARERS, LONG, RESTING
ON SEAT TRACK ON TOP BOAT

LONG CHAIN SLING

SHORT CHAIN SLING

BOAT CRADLE

Note:
Canvas cover
not shown

Fig. #1:

The Stormboat Transport
(Not To Scale)

They had watched helplessly as their trucks made the turn and the others did not. Someone would have to go after them, but the jeeps were in the orchard and blocked from pursuing their lost colleagues. With no way to move the immobilized vehicle forward or backward, Lieutenants Martin and Kennedy, conscious that time was critical if the evacuation was to take place under the cover of darkness, made the decision to tip the truck into the ditch to allow the rest of the convoy to proceed to the staging area. With the bridge open, the other trucks drove into the orchard, drove along the trees to the winter dyke, turned left and parked between the trees and the dyke. Major Tucker had no choice but to wait until all the trucks were in the orchard and off the bridge before he sent an officer in a jeep to retrieve the three trucks that had gone astray.

Lieutenant John Cronyn was the one that went after the wayward men. He recalled: *'Once all the Storm boats and trucks*

Unloading

Unloading Instructions:

1) Remove canvas covers, chain sling short and steel trough ramps from top boat.

2) Remove rear support.

3) Roll lorry canvas cover and use this to protect the bottom of boat when unloading. Detach chain sling long from cradle and use to pull boats down slides of cradle, stopping when they reach the point of balance. See Fig. #2. This may either be done by hand, about 8 men being required or by anchoring the chain to another lorry or a tree and driving the loaded lorry slowly forward. On reaching the point of balance the boats shall be lowered gently onto the canvas cover.

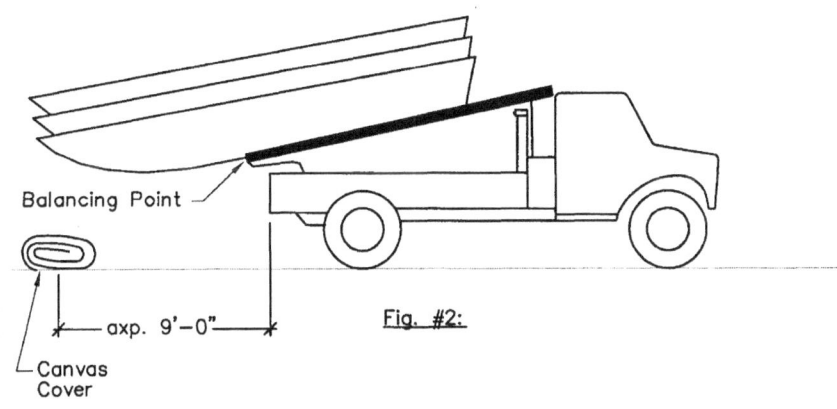

Balancing Point

axp. 9'—0"

Canvas Cover

Fig. #2:

4) Slowly drive lorry forward allowing the stern to slowly drop.
5) Proceed to unload the boats singly.

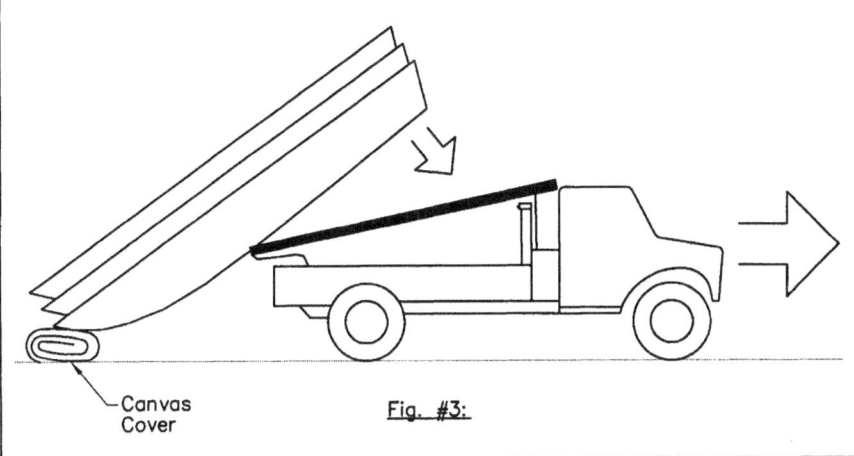

Canvas Cover

Fig. #3:

were in the orchard, I went back in a jeep to find the three person-
nel lorries and lead them up. By this time it was very dark and,

as the road was a very treacherous one to follow, I felt it necessary to put on my rear axle light in order that the three lorries could follow me into the orchard. As we came back along the road, the German 88's opened up on us and were too close for comfort! I looked back to see if I could see the lorries following me and actually saw an 88 shell ricochet off the road in a shower of sparks between the jeep and the truck following me, without exploding. It went into the next field where it finally did explode. It was apparent that the Germans were able to see even our small axle lights and were firing at us over open sights. However, we made it to the orchard and the men went to work by getting the boats off-loaded and the engines on, with the slow, difficult job of moving them down to the river. It was an incredibly difficult job to get them up and over the winter dyke, which was very muddy and slippery. I left the off-loaders in the orchard and went on over the winter dyke and over the summer dyke to the edge of the river." [50]

The additional men recovered by Lieutenant Cronyn were quickly put to work unloading boats. The trucks with the Storm boats had already driven through the orchard and were positioned as close to the winter dyke as possible before unloading the boats.

Hand ropes and a guide tape were fixed along the route. Without hesitation the boats started to be off loaded. It required 8 men to unload each boat. From a position just behind the dyke, the maintenance party from the 10th Field Park Company, RCE unpacked, tested and mounted the engines onto the boats. When they were ready and fueled, the boats were on their way. Due to the darkness and confined space in the staging area all the platoons were mixed together and sappers had to follow orders from unknown NCOs. This situation might have caused serious delays in the operation had it not been for the strong leadership demonstrated by the officers and NCOs of the 23rd. Major Tucker recalled: *"This mishap was unfortunate, as all available personnel had to be called up to get on with the job and there was never an opportunity to segregate one platoon from another. The effectiveness of many NCO was nullified and a far greater burden was thrown on those responsible for directing operations than would have been the case had the NCOs been in control of their own men. It is doubtful, though, if this detracted from the success of the operation, since everyone was quick to respond to orders given by the man in charge of the job."* [51]

The man responsible for getting the boats off the tracks and down to the river was Lieutenant Kennedy. The burden on his shoulders was increased as the rain softened ground turned it to greasy mud, churned up by the men's feet. Under his leadership, the carrying parties struggled with the heavy boats through the muddy orchard to the base of their first obstacle: the winter dyke.

The Assignments

Major Tucker decided to direct operations from his command post on the beach on the south bank of the river and Lieutenant Kennedy was to expedite delivery of the boats the best way that he could. He was to sort out difficulties in the boat delivery operation and keep the line moving. With terrain that was challenging enough in the daylight, and an enemy who was constantly shelling the area, it would not be an easy task. Kennedy's second-in-command was Lieutenant Tate, who was to assist him in any way possible.

Lieutenants Martin and Cronyn were to take their usual assignments to control the loading operations from opposite banks of the river, Lieutenant Martin on the north and Lieutenant Cronyn on the south bank. This was a procedure that they had perfected during the Seine crossings. A refueling point was to be set up on the south shore, one hundred yards from the launch site, under the command of Sergeant George King of Truro, Nova Scotia. Sergeant King was also tasked with taking charge of the marshalling site for the reverse boats. These were to be the Storm boats that would be immediately put into service whenever a boat needed to be refueled. It was expected that during the course of the evening some of the boats would develop engine problems and while being repaired, the boats in reverse would take their place.

It was understood by Major Tucker that all of the wounded in the Oosterbeek pocket would be left so as to not delay the evacuation, which had only one night to withdraw as many of the surviving 1st Airborne soldiers as possible. However, General Urquhart was unwilling to abandon any of the wounded who were able to make it to the evacuation site. He therefore made allowances for the walking wounded to be evacuated as well, even though it added to the risk that not all the troops would be evacuated under the cover of darkness. Although this change in how the wounded would be treated was not communicated to the 23rd, Major Tucker fortunately had the foresight to order an aid post set up in the culvert of the summer dyke. Lance Corporal Roseborough and Sapper E.S. MacDonald were detailed to set up the aid post and assist the wounded that Tucker knew would inevitably appear.

Part of 1 Platoon: Back row l to r, J.D. Hubburd, Norman 'Moose' Caldwell. Front row l to r: L/Cpl. Ben Watling, Sidney Smith and Charlie Thorton. (Luuk Buist)

Getting To The Water

A report submitted by Colonel C.J. Bermingham, dated 26 October 1944 showed the results of a test that had been conducted using five different methods to transport Storm boats to and over dykes. Sixteen to eighteen men per boat tried to carry or drag a boat 100 yards and then up and over a 12 foot dyke. The most effective method was using 1½ inch steel pipe carrying bars slid into 3/8 inch iron loops welded to the boats. Simply carrying the boats proved to be the slowest and most exhausting means of transportation. Unfortunately, this was the only available method that the men of the 23rd Field Company, RCE had at the time of Operation Berlin. Even worse, they had to haul the 14 heavy boats up and over a winter dike of 18-20 feet, then over a summer dyke of 7-10 feet and then down to the water, a distance of 500 yards in total. The slopes of these winter dykes were at approximately a 45-degree angle, which quickly exhausted the hauling parties, while those of the summer dykes were not nearly as steep.

The other engineer companies had to cross similar terrain but the Assault boats that the two British engineer companies had to carry were smaller and lighter. A group of twelve or so sappers could carry the boat on their shoulders to the river. It wasn't an easy task, but compared to handling the bulkier and heavier Storm boats, it allowed them to be in position to launch their boats earlier. The 20th Field Company, RCE had the same problems as the 23rd did, but with two additional dykes, called flood banks, to cross. Besides having fewer boats to move, the only advantage that they had was that they brought more men to help carry them.

Their first obstacle, which was also the worst, was the winter dyke. It was so steep that men had to practically crawl up on the wet grass to get over it. Lieutenant Kennedy commented on his first trip over: *It was unbelievably difficult to climb the winter dyke and we left men to fix hand ropes over it...*[52]

Even with the hand ropes, the men still struggled to get

themselves and the boats up the wet slippery slope. Not an easy task with boats which Sergeant George King claimed, *"must have weighed at least 1200 pounds."* [53]

Corporal Robinson led the first carrying party as they somehow got the heavy boat and themselves up and over the dyke. Their feet had churned the ground up, leaving hardly any footing for the next crew who followed in their wake. Added to the rain and the darkness was the great noise and intensity of the barrage by the guns of the 94th, 112th and 179th Field Regiments, Royal Artillery, which commenced firing at 2100 hours. Sergeant George Willick remembered: *"All you could see was nothing but the flash of artillery and mortar shells."* [54]   At first, this frightened many of the sappers as they were working in the orchards. They didn't realize that it was their own guns firing. Slowly, they relaxed as they realized it was fire support from XXX Corps designed to engage the enemy surrounding the pocket at Oosterbeek and allow the Airborne evacuees to withdraw over the river unnoticed. This barrage was designed to mask the sounds of the retreating airborne troops by keeping the enemies' heads down and it also covered the sound of the Storm boat engines. However, due to ammunition shortages, the barrage never reached the crescendo necessary to fully drown out all noises from the engines.

With the Allied barrage landing just outside of the perimeter, the Germans thought that a further relief force was attempting to cross the Neder Rijn and thus brought their guns into action. Soon, everyone seemed to be firing into the shadows. Lieutenant John Cronyn described the scene this way: *"By this time all hell had broken loose. Not only was our supporting barrage going overhead with a thunderous roar, but the Germans were firing back with great vigour, using 88s, "moaning minnies", normal mortars and machine guns. This was the first time moaning minnies had been fired at us and I must say they made a very disconcerting noise and had a great capacity to terrify people."'* [55]
`Moaning Minnies' was the name that Allied soldiers gave to the German rocket artillery, or Nebelwerfer, which was used as an area weapon. The noise produced by the Nebelwerfer was de-

scribed by one Canadian soldier as a series of *"groans, howls whines, like baying hounds for 10 to 15 seconds; then [they] grow louder and louder and finally burst with one hell of a blast."*[56]

Fortunately, most of the shelling was down at the beach area so as not to be too much of a hindrance to the men preparing and struggling with the boats. Every so often, however, the enemy artillery would target the dykes and the orchard beyond. This had a bad effect on the carrying parties, which would drop their boats and duck for cover. This resulted in some damage, later found on the first craft, which had been dropped on rocks scattered along the path. Also, according to Donald Somerville: *"The Germans were firing machine guns at us, the tracers bouncing off the dike wall seemed to go right through your legs';* another incentive to drop the boat and dive for cover."[57]

Sapper Clayton Moss admitted he was frightened: *"If you weren't scared, you were nuts."* He remembered that he was on edge all night, *"you had to freeze every time a shell landed so you wouldn't be spotted by the enemy spotters. I didn't see anything until an explosion lit the area up. And some of them were closer than you thought or were comfortable with."* Then he added again, *"If you weren't scared, you were nuts."*[58] He wasn't the only one that was deeply affected by this night. Until the day he died, Sapper Moose Caldwell had nightmares about what happened that night.

What appeared to be chaotic activity added to the tension caused by the shelling, but everyone did his best to carry out his assigned task. Lieutenant John Cronyn stated that: *"One of the great difficulties of the operation was the fact that only our two reconnaissance officers, Lieutenant R.J. Kennedy and R.S. Tate, had actually seen the whole site in daylight. The rest of us were operating without any idea of the terrain at all, other than from the maps we had seen in a very brief "O" group before proceeding from Valburg. White tapes had been laid to the operational site and I followed these to take up my usual position as officer in charge of operating the boats from the assault side".*[59]

Lieutenant Cronyn was able to determine the boundaries of the crossing area with the help of tracers from two 40mm Bofors

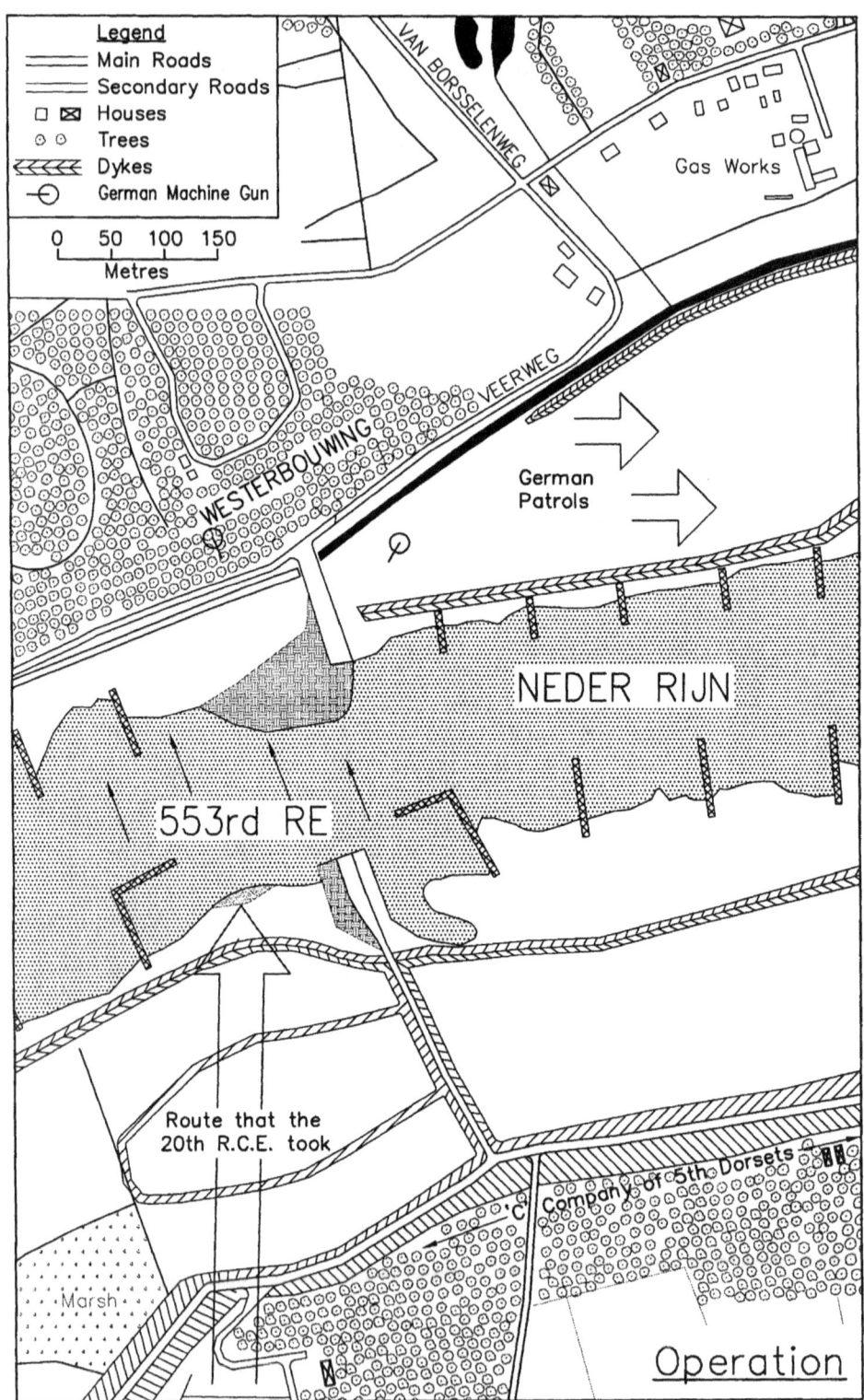

Legend
- Main Roads
- Secondary Roads
- ☐ ⊠ Houses
- ◦ ◦ Trees
- Dykes
- German Machine Gun

0   50   100   150
Metres

VAN BORSSELENWEG

Gas Works

VEERWEG

WESTERBOUWING

German
Patrols

NEDER RIJN

553rd RE

Route that the
20th R.C.E. took

"C" Company of 5th Dorsets

Marsh

Operation

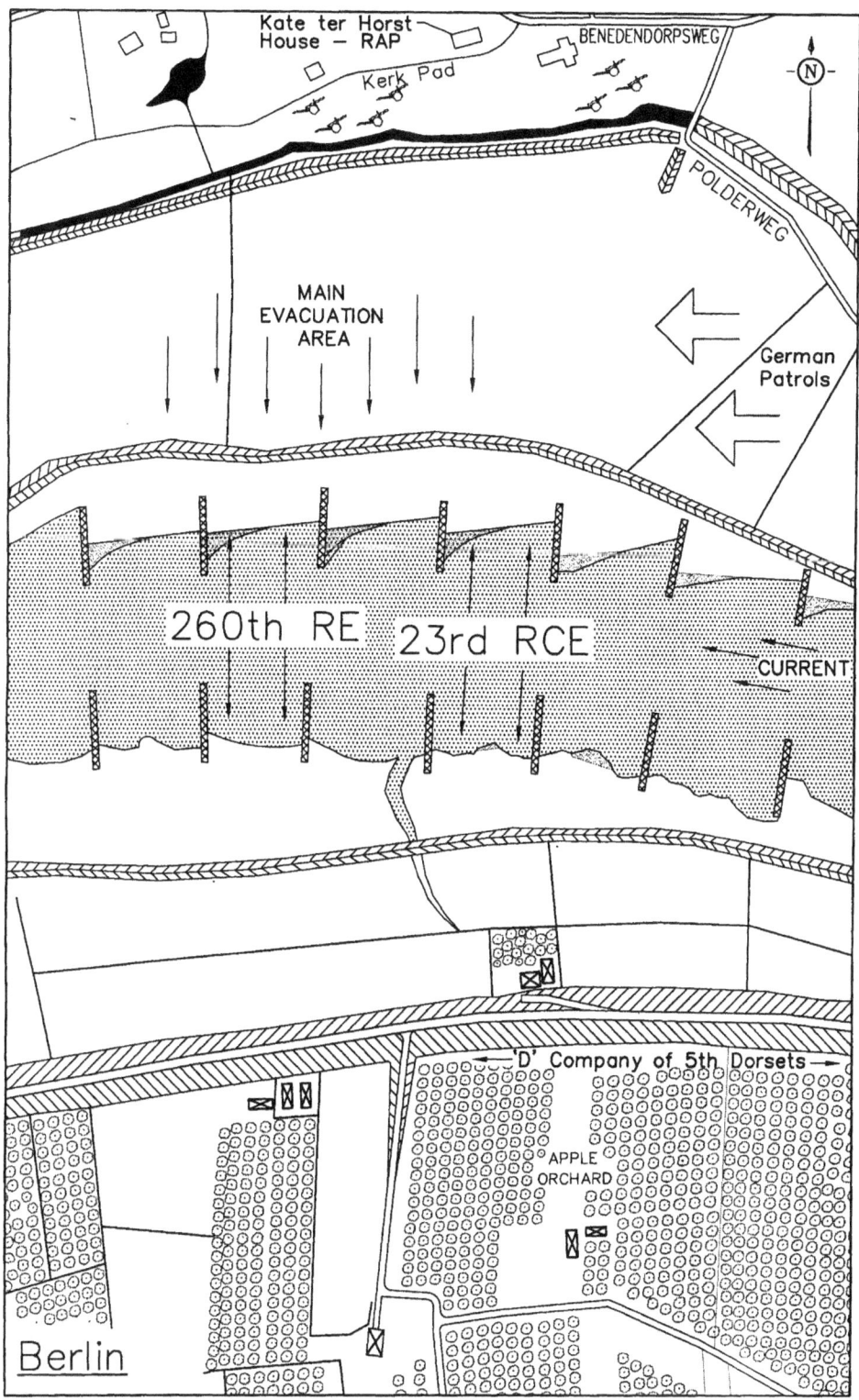

guns of the 110th Light Anti-aircraft Regiment. The tracers were shot into the sky over the river to act as guiding beacons. A gun was placed at each end to mark the flanks of the evacuation area.

After overcoming the difficult winter dyke, it was roughly a quarter of a mile down to the summer dyke. This obstacle was 7 to 10 feet high and the slopes were not as severe as the winter dyke. After the summer dyke was crossed it was a hundred more yards through the mud to the river's edge.

A small mud beach about twenty yards wide was used to launch the boats. A larger beach - about sixty yards wide - was used to service the boats and this was where Major Tucker set up his command post. Separating the two beaches was a groin built of rock projecting about 30 yards into the river.

Another complication that affected the boats was the groins that had been built on both sides of the river at this point. These groins were used to speed up the current where silt tended to build up and create problems for shipping. However, they had an interesting effect on the current. The current would squeeze around the end of the groin causing a partial cross-current for a short distance. This irregularity caused problems for any boat that operated near them. With one of these structures every 150 yards or so along this stretch of the river, the course of every boat launched this night was affected.

Through sheer determination, Corporal Robinson's crew delivered their Storm boat loaded with a 4-cylinder 50 HP motor, spare gas and paddles by 2130 hours. They did this in the rain and darkness while under enemy fire. Regardless of the difficulties, the first of the boats and crew made the 500 yard journey from the orchard to the river—but the journey from the staging area in the orchard had taken a huge toll on the boat.

2

The Non-attack Attack

In an effort to confuse the German forces as to the true intent of the activities on the Lower Rhine the night 25/26 September, parts of the 43rd Wessex Division staged a mock attack at Renkum, 6 kilometres west of Oosterbeek. This was approximately the same area where General Horrocks had intended to launch the divisional sized bridgehead across the Neder Rijn, if the Dorsets' crossing had been successful on the previous night. This ad hoc formation was centered on the 43rd Reconnaissance Regiment, which was deployed along that section of the river—not the 129th Infantry Brigade originally assigned the task, as stated in the divisional war diary. In addition the regiment's armoured and un-armoured vehicles there were DUKWs and Royal Engineers' trucks containing bridging equipment. The plan was for the column to approach the Neder Rijn at dusk and while under enemy observation deploy their forces to simulate a river crossing. It was hoped that the Germans on the west side of the Oosterbeek perimeter, the von Tettau Division, would focus on this apparent river assault and allow the evacuation to go uncontested.

The 43rd's War Diary stated: *"This consisted of a motley column of mortar and carrier platoons, a machine gun platoon, a number of empty DUKWS, pontoon and bridge lorries under control of 5 Wilts.* (5th Bn., The Wiltshire Regiment of the 129th Infantry Brigade). *As dusk approached, it moved ostentatiously to the village of Heteren on the banks of the river and opened up for one hour with Bren guns, machine guns and mortars on the far bank. This deception undoubtedly...contributed to the success of the withdrawal."* [60]

Lieutenant-General Hans von Tettau was in the process of moving his command post that night and misread all the reports concerning the activities along the south bank. In fact, very few commanders of the various Kampfgruppe (combat groups) surrounding the pocket entertained the thought of a mass evacuation by their foe. Those who detected the increased activity on the southern bank and boat traffic on the river dismissed it as another attempt to re-supply the pocket, or as isolated break-outs. The great fear for the Germans remained an amphibious assault from the south bank like the one envisioned by Brigadier General Horrocks on the 24th. So the German counter-barrage throughout the night was a reaction to the perceived threat of Allied aggression, rather than the actual withdrawal.

The Western Site

(553rd R.E. and the 20th R.C.E.)

It had been assumed that the previous night's operation had been successful and that the 4th Battalion of the Dorsetshire Regiment, which had been sent over, had taken the Westerbou-wing heights, thus widening the bridgehead north of the river. Unfortunately, they had failed to do so. What was even more tragic was that no one on the south bank had realized this be-cause communications with the battalion had never been estab-lished. When the decision was made to establish a second evacuation site with equal resources, men and boats were drawn away from the primary evacuation site where their efforts would have produced better results.

Lieutenant W.W. Gemmell was a platoon leader for the 20th Field Company, RCE. He described what he witnessed: *"We waited in the orchard until dark and then in close behind the dyke. The storm boats and motors were ready to go. All we had to do was get them over the dyke and down to the river. I made the initial recce. You couldn't just walk across that dyke. Jerry had, I'd say, about six or seven M.G.'s on the north bank; you had to spot the tracers and duck over when they went past. I couldn't see any signals from the paratroopers opposite our position but I did notice several flashes, presumably from flash lights, further up the river opposite the 23rd Field."* [61]

When the 20th Field Company, RCE and their eight Storm Boats were unloaded in the orchard, they met the same problems that the 23rd Field Company, RCE had with the slippery mud on the winter and summer dykes. In addition the 20th Field Com-

There are no known photos of Operation Berlin so these are photographs from other operations. Top: Sappers from the 3rd Canadian Infantry Division man-handle a Storm boat during Operation Duck. (PA138285 Library and Archives Canada) Below: A member of the 23rd Field Company, R.C.E. holds the front of a Storm boat as soldiers of the 101st Airborne Division exit onto the south bank of the Waal River as they were being evacuated off The Island in November 1944. By this point the 23rd were well practised in Storm boat operations and a few months later they set up a school at the Nijmegen power station to train other units in how to properly handle Storm boats.

pany, RCE had to cope with the extra features of two flood banks and two fences. On the top of the winter dyke was a 12 foot wide road bordered on each shoulder by a fence made of three strands of thick wire, which had to be cut, and an iron post had to be removed to allow the Storm boats to pass. Sapper Harry Decker Thickie of the 20th Field Company, RCE bent the wires on the first fence so many times that it broke and then started on the fence on the north side of the road. He even removed the iron port with a shovel, all this while the Germans sent up flares, exposing his position to machine gun fire. He then helped carry the first boat to the river and volunteered to crew the boat across the Neder Rijn. The personal risks he took that night to ensure the Storm boats could gain access to the river, along with the further risks he took throughout the night, earned him the Military Medal.

Lance Corporal Norman Dalmar of Petersfield, Manitoba in 1 Platoon of 20th Field Company, RCE said: *"It seemed like forever before we reached the river on account of flares, machine gun fire and mortars coming in, the boat was put down several times. You had to be there to realize the chaotic situation. Across the river and to our left, buildings at the water's edge were burning. Also German machine gun and mortar fire was coming in from that area. Many people were swimming or floating on whatever would give them buoyancy. Also they were fully clothed or partially. One chap was almost nude."* [62]

The 20th Field Company, RCE wasn't having much luck. Their OC, Major A.W. Jones, attributed this to, *"incessant machine gun fire from three enemy posts on the far bank directly opposite the site, it was decided between the R.E.'s and ourselves that it would not be practical to immediately start up Evinrude motors and consequently give our position away. It was then decided to send an assault boat across to make a recce and to ascertain the number of troops waiting on the far bank. Also to hinder our progress and make it more hazardous, a large factory was burning furiously and lit up our side of the river!"* [63]

The first Assault boat of the 553rd Field Company, RE, with Sergeant Petrie in charge, was put in the water at 21:30 hours.

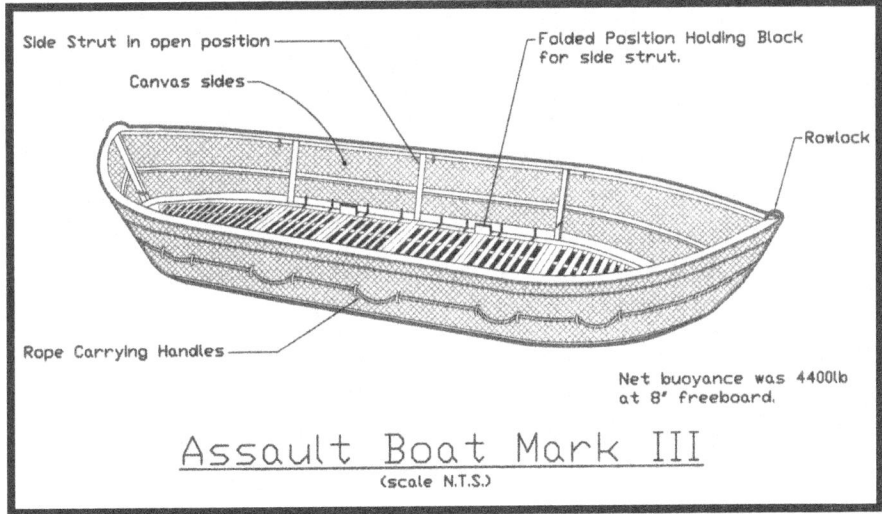

Side Strut in open position

Canvas sides

Folded Position Holding Block for side strut.

Rowlock

Rope Carrying Handles

Net buoyance was 4400lb at 8' freeboard.

Assault Boat Mark III
(scale N.T.S.)

Ten minutes later, after braving the enemy fire from the heights, it was on the north bank. Sergeant Petrie's boat came back with only two men of the Dorsets, who had been hiding in an abandoned DUKW from the previous night's crossing, but no Airborne men. Another boat was sent and it also came back without any evacuees. At 2330 hours Sergeant Petrie made a second crossing even though he knew that the Germans were alert and in strength on the north shore, and also failed to find any survivors. For his actions, which set an example for the men in his unit, Sergeant Petrie earned the Military Medal. However, a section of resourceful men of the Dorset Regiment found an abandoned Assault boat from the previous night's operations on the north bank and used it to safely cross the river.

After temporarily abandoning operations at 0100 hours because of the beach being shelled by mortars from the 43rd Wessex Division that fell short of their mark, another Assault boat was dispatched at 0200 hrs and it came back with two more stragglers.

At 0300 hours the evacuation was called off in this area. The intensity of machine gun and mortar fire would not allow the engineers to operate in an exposed position. Four Storm boats and all of the motors were removed to the flood bank. At 0330 hours orders were given to send the four Storm boats to the site 1,500 yards to the right where the 23rd Field Company, RCE were operating. This meant re-launching the boats, which entailed carrying them back over the flood banks, the summer dyke and through the mud. As they were re-launching, one boat was hit by mortar fire and sank. A second boat made it halfway up the river before machine gun fire forced it to take cover on the south bank. This is where the motor failed, and it was abandoned. The crew struggled to safety through mud that was up to their hips. The other two boats were not launched as it was nearing daylight, and the enemy had this section of the river covered with machine guns, so the risk was too great.

A total of 48 evacuees came through the western site, mainly using Assault boats. The 553rd War Diary says that it brought back about 25 men while, despite their efforts, the 20th Field Company, RCE were not able to evacuate any men in four separate crossings. Fortunately, no casualties were reported during their futile and dangerous mission. However, some evacuees had landed in the area of operations of the 20th; the 553rd had launched their Assault boats at the eastern site and had been swept downstream.

Lieutenant Gemmel supports this theory. He said: *"I'll never forget those British paratroopers. They had taken the hell of a kicking around for ten days but were still full of the old ginger. Lots of them came downstream to our area from the 23rd's, and got into some farmhouses; of course, out came the old tea, which brewed up into the best drink I ever had in my life, bar none."* [64]

One of those men who found their own way into their area was Private Wilf `Ginger' Oldham of the Border Regiment, though it is questionable who supplied the tea. His story is typical of a lot of guys who came through the 20th Field Company's area. He said, *"In the dark the river seemed miles wide and very fast flowing and although I could swim I was certain I would never make the opposite shore...I think about ten of us set off, suddenly on the bank was a rowing boat with I think three or four oars. I got hold of one oar although I had never rowed before and off we set. The strong current took us some part down the river, then the opposite bank. We had to wade in the narrows towards the tracer shells, this we did almost by light then, dug in a slit trench a soldier said, something like, come on lads , you're safe now. Up a little bunch, we got split up now and after a short while I was greeted by Canadian voices who told us to sit down and wait as one of them brought me a mug of tea, the first hot drink that I had in days."* [65]

The Eastern Site

Phase One: the 260th RE

Brigadier Essame of the 43rd Wessex Division described the start of the evacuation: "*At nine o'clock, the whole divisional artillery opened up with overwhelming effect, tracers from the LAA Regiment marking the flanks of the crossings, A and C Companies of 8 Middlesex thickened up the fire [with heavy mortars and MMGs]. The noise was deafening and awesome as the first parties of Sappers carried the assault boats over the dyke walls and down to the water's edge. The crews dipped their oars and disappeared into the darkness. More boats followed. Punctually at 9:40 p.m. the first reached the far side and waited for the Airborne troops who were due at ten."* [66]

Lieutenant Alan Bevan and sappers from the 260th Field Company, RE were the first to arrive on the north bank. To get to the assigned spot, they had to paddle diagonally against the strong current. The river was in near-flood conditions after all the recent rains so it took them roughly ten minutes of intense paddling to cross. This was an eternity compared to the powered Storm boat's crossing time of three minutes.

Lieutenant Bevan stayed on the north bank for two hours, directing the loading of soldiers into the 16 Assault boats manned by the 260th Field Company, RE. For his outstanding display of courage and leadership during the night, Lieutenant Bevan was awarded the Military Cross.

If it seemed to be an eternity crossing over in an Assault boat then time must have seemed like it was running backwards for Lieutenant-Colonel Henniker. Being the architect of this plan made him fully aware of the pitfalls that may occur. He recalls, "*Within a few minutes there were several canvas assault boats launched. They vanished into the inky darkness. There was nothing to be seen and nothing seemed to be happening. I paced the shore concealing, I hope, the inevitable doubts that assailed me. Had the Sappers upset the boats and all gone silently to the bottom? Had they paddled their boats into waiting Germans, concealed on the far bank? Had the boats been washed downstream to God knows where? It was a tense interval and no man could have importuned his Maker more fervently than I did that night. I do not know how long the interval was, but perhaps after ten to fifteen minutes, though it seemed longer, there came across the darkness the sound of dipping paddles. Then I saw a boat. It held a dozen men. I could recognize their airborne-pattern helmets. What a welcome sight it was. First one boat, then another, then another. About sixty men, including many wounded, came ashore."* [67]

"The Airborne Troops were very pleased to see us," records the 260th war diary.[68] The soldiers who greeted the first assault boats coming to evacuate them were a far cry from the men who had landed north of the Neder Rijn over a week earlier. They were tired, hungry and dirty from the continuous battle they had been fighting with few supplies. To prevent detection by the Germans on the way to the evacuation site the soldiers had been instructed to blacken their faces and wrap their boots in cloth strips to muffle noise. Even with the physical discomforts they experienced over the past nine days and the driving rain that saturated their uniforms, the Airborne soldiers' stoic professionalism shone through. They waited patiently in a queue for their turn to cross the river to safety and allowed the wounded to be evacuated first.

The wounded, both those walking wounded from the Regimental Aid Post (RAP) and those wounded on the way to the evacuation site, were given priority. This caused delays in loading the boats and helps to explain the long delays in their return to the south bank which had so worried Lieutenant Colonel Henniker. Because the sappers had been previously briefed that no wounded were to be evacuated, there were occasional incidents where they baulked at taking the wounded out. Sergeant Jock

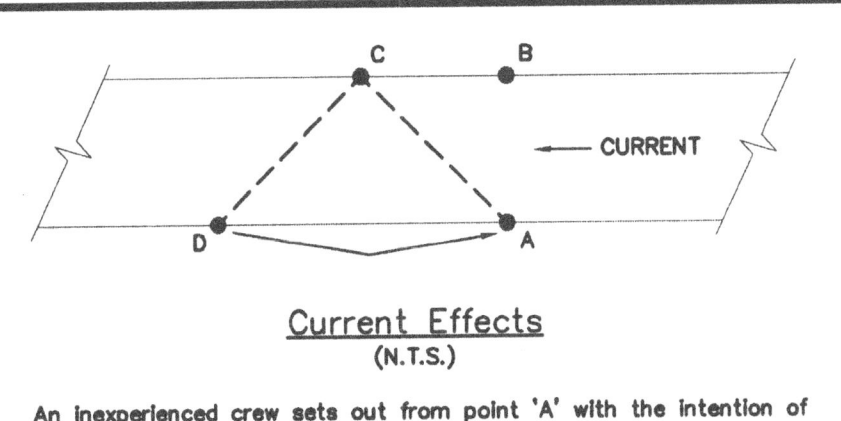

Current Effects
(N.T.S.)

An inexperienced crew sets out from point 'A' with the intention of landing at point 'B'. However, the strong current carries them to point 'C'. On their return trip, the current carries them further downstream and they wind up at point 'D'. Before their next launch, the boats must be carried back to point 'A'.

East, in an effort to get one of his wounded comrades loaded onto an Assault boat, was forced to, *"threatened them with my rifle and bayonet and as we got Jim into a boat. I held on to the side as I did not want them to think that Jim was taking my place."* [69] Events like this were exceedingly rare as the night progressed and the boat crews realized that the Airborne were not about to abandon any wounded that could reach the evacuation site.

Eight Assault boats were launched to start the operation and as had been the experience of the previous night, due to the strong current, an Assault boat had little chance of going directly across the river and hitting its target. Most boats were carried downstream, perhaps as much as 200 yards and another 200 yards on the return trip. That could put them 400 yards from their starting point. If that happened then the boats had to be carried back to the starting point in order to be relaunched successfully. This is confirmed by Lieutenant-Colonel Henniker's comment: *"The boats were hauled back to the starting point for another trip."* [70]

Two other men from this unit were to be recognized for their bravery during the night: Sergeant Fred Hilton, who spent three hours helping to organize the evacuation on the north bank; and Sapper Arthur Denmark, who made over twenty crossings of the

Neder Rijn evacuating Airborne troops. Both men received the Military Medal for their bravery and were an inspiration to their fellow soldiers on that daunting night.

Lt-Col. Henniker must have relaxed a little because so far all appeared to be going as planned. The 260th Field Company, RE had made contact with the 1st Airborne and had started the flow of men out of the besieged perimeter. Now it was time for phase two.

Phase Two: A Rough Start

A few hundred yards east, the British sappers were joined by the 23rd Field Company, RCE. Their plan was to use the same procedures during the evacuation as the ones they used in training and the crossing of the Seine River. Lieutenant Russ Kennedy described how they operated Storm boats: *"In order to get an assault wave of boats off across a river, we put a crew of three in each boat. The operators would start motors while the bow was held on shore by the two crewman. On signal, one section of infantry would pile in over each blunt bow; the crewman would push the loaded boat backwards into deeper water against the thrust of the throttled-down motor, and then try to tumble in themselves as the operators turned the craft outwards for the crossing. An awkward drill, but it worked, and we could move troops across a river at 50 to 100 men per boat per hour, depending on the width* [of the river]." [71]

This awkward technique was necessary because the Evinrude engines did not have a reverse gear, which meant the crew had to re-orient the boat towards open water before the engine could be fully engaged. The first Storm boat was launched around 21:30 and promptly started to sink within a few feet of the shoreline. It was immediately hauled out of the river and placed out of the way, so it wouldn't become an obstacle to boats trying to dock in the dark. It was soon discovered that the boat had been damaged while it had been carried down to the launch site. Major Tucker commented that it was found to have *"been badly holed when the men carrying it slipped down the side of the floodwall and the stream of water which poured into it would have sunk it before it could completed a crossing."* [72]

Quickly, men were assigned to clear the path of rocks and to help bring up another boat without damaging it. By 2145 hours, the second Storm boat was launched. The crew consisted of Corporal Ryan and Sappers Magnusson and Roherty. Their first passenger was one of their own. It was Lieutenant Russ Martin, who was assigned the task of going over to organize the loading on the north side of the river. Lieutenant-Colonel Henniker saw the boat as it disappeared into the darkness: *"More and more boats (assault boats of the 260th) were launched and then I heard the first Canadian Storm boat's motor start. First it spluttered, then it roared. Then a boat with a white, foaming, wake was visible aiming for the far bank.'"* [73] It got no further than mid-river when, according to several witnesses, the craft was blown apart by a direct hit from a mortar. There were no survivors. With the loss of Lieutenant Martin, the 23rd did not have a liaison officer to coordinate the withdrawal on the north bank. However, Major Tucker was not to know this for some hours due to the chaos generated by the evacuation, and very little could be seen on the river. The only light came from the fires burning in Oosterbeek, the factory down the river in Heavendrop or from the exploding shells landing in and around the embarkment area. Lieutenant Kennedy remembers: *"The stray light from the fires reflected from the clouds should have helped a little but we did a lot of groping* [in the dark]." [74] Sergeant Sandy Morris of Trinity, Newfoundland agreed: *"The view was terribly bad. You couldn't see anything. The men in the boats weren't totally sure where they were going. You couldn't show them a signal light for the Germans to zero in on."* [75]

The 23rd Field Company, RCE War Diary records that a German mortar was observed firing directly opposite the launching site while the first four boats were being launched. After that it was not seen again and Major Tucker presumed that the 1st Airborne troops in the bridgehead must have cleared it up. Even though light from the burning factory in Heavendrop penetrated the darkness it was still very difficult to determine distances. Since there were no reports by the British 1st Airborne Division of a mortar being engaged that night, what he saw must have come from a German position further inland, which most likely shelled Lieutenant Martin's boat.

At 2215 hours, the third boat, commanded by Corporal McLachlan with Sappers Harold Barr and A.C. Thomas on board, was launched and, like the second, it disappeared into the darkness and only the sound of its engine could be heard. Twenty minutes later, the fourth boat was in the water with Corporal Smith and Sappers Hope and Thompson on board. Corporal Smith followed the path of the other two boats, looking in the darkness for people to evacuate. Then nothing happened. Besides the shelling, the weather and the constant fire of machine guns, it was quiet. No engines were heard.

It had been 50 minutes since the second Storm boat had disappeared into the night, 65 minutes since the failed first launch and there was still no sign of any returning boats loaded with Airborne troops. Major Tucker was concerned about the delay and although he must have been happy to see that the 260th Field Company, RE was having success, he was worried about his own men.

Finally, the third boat returned, with Corporal McLachlan in charge. It had been delayed because most of the men they brought back were wounded and loading had gone slowly. These men might have been the remainders of the 50 wounded men that Padre Watkins and two medical orderlies helped down from Kate ter Horst's house. All of the thirty men that they took had made it to safety and were well taken care of on the south bank thanks to the Roman-Catholic priest, Father Mongeon, who helped the sappers carry the wounded to the aid station on improvised stretchers made from the men's great coats.

With his boat empty, Corporal McLachlan and his crew went back for more men and soon came with another boatload of wounded men. Sergeant Sandy Morris was on the beach and described what he saw: *"The boats that came back were mostly full of wounded. We carried the wounded from the boats and laid them on the ground with nothing to cover them. The rain was dreadful!"* [76]

Steadily, those who waited were rescued and the wounded men were unloaded on the south bank. The stretcher teams had trouble keeping up with the unloading. On the beach, Lieutenant John Cronyn remembers trying to comfort a badly wounded paratrooper while waiting for a stretcher to pick him up: *"I kept assuring him that he was safe, despite the shelling, mortaring and machine gunning that was going on at the time. But really, by comparison with what he had gone through on the other side, he was safe."* [77]

The Aid Station became busier than they had expected. The engineers had been told that they could expect only unwounded troops. They only had the usual First Aid resources to deal with a company of men, not a division of men who had been receiving wounds for nine days. As more and more boatloads of wounded men arrived, it was now becoming impossible to deal with all of the wounded. By the end of the night L/Cpl. Rosebrough and Sapper E.S. MacDonald had treated sixty-nine stretcher cases and over a hundred walking wounded, some of them their own. Some men, who could find the strength, helped the less seriously wounded. Everyone did the best they could under the overwhelming circumstances. After their initial treatment at the 23rd's aid post, the evacuation of the wounded was the responsibility of the 130 Field Ambulance of the 43rd Division who had a Car Post set up in the orchard. From there they were evacuated to the Company Command Post (CCP) at Driel, and finally to the Advanced Dressing Station (ADS) at Valburg in a fleet of jeep ambulances. The members of the 551st G.T. Company, once their trucks were empty of Storm boats, helped transport the wounded back to the hospital in Driel. Also helping were the drivers of the 3-ton lorries of the 5th Battalion, The Dorset Regiment.

Lieutenant Colonel Myers was in overall control of the evacuation on the north bank, although he had co-opted various officers to assist in controlling the loading of individual boats, with the priority on evacuating the wounded first. One such officer was Lieutenant Colonel Preston, the 1st Airborne Division's principal administrative officer who stated: *"The walking wounded were helped and hauled over the side to lie in the bottom*

Above: A 1930 photograph looking north across the Neder Rijn into Oosterbeek. The old church is just right of centre. The 23rd Field Company, R.C.E. operated directly across from the church or at least that was its intention. (Rober Voskuil)

Below: The view that the German machine gunners had from the top of the Westerbouwing. In broad daylight any moment would have been an easy target. This is an old Dutch prewar postcard. (Robert Voskuil)

amongst the boats of the others. The air was full of whispered curses and mutterings of those getting aboard and of the blasphemies of the crews who had the two fold task of preventing the boat being swamped by its passengers and bearing hold by the boulders on the bank. For a moment the boat had filled with men, and those still trying to clamber in were prevented from doing so by those already there, failing to climb aboard were falling into the water or onto the shore." [78] In an urgent whisper Colonel Preston ordered the men to wait for the next boat. For the first time, rank didn't matter. Whoever he was, the next man in line was the next onto the boats. One of them was Major General Urquhart who was waiting to make the crossing, taking orders from those in charge just like his soldiers: *"Eddie Myers moved about the bank embarking parties as rapidly as he could and Mackenzie, who had slipped off to see what was happening at the other crossing point, returned to tell me that the delay we were now experiencing was due to the sinking of something like half of the boats within the first hour. As these losses were understandably not distributed equally between the two crossings, some reorganization had been necessary. And as Myers now did his best to compensate for the lost craft by swift turn rounds and efficient loading, soldiers lay in the churned ground whispering witticisms. A mortar bomb landed some twenty yards away. Another followed. The chugging of the storm boats' engines sounded alarmingly loud and now and then we could hear splashing as men scrambled aboard, or started to swim from sinking craft. Then, from out of the night came a subdued voice: `Right - this party,' I looked at my watch. It was a few minutes past midnight. We collected ourselves and slid down the banking. By the light of the tracer I could see other boats dimly through the rain. I climbed aboard from the sodden, slippery groin. It was a squeeze and the boat was low in the water. There was an exclamation from the Canadian sapper who was running this ferry, and from the disgusted tone it was plain that all was not well. We had, in fact, gotten stuck in the mud. Someone slipped over the side to push us off. It was my diminutive batman, Hancock. He got us clear as the boat moved slowly out and into the deeper water Han-*

cock was still holding on. He struggled to get aboard again and some other occupant shouted down to him: 'Let go! It's over-crowded already.' Irked by such ingratitude, Hancock ignored the remark and summoning his last reserves pulled himself into the boat." [79]

The General observed splashes in the water from German machine guns and thought that the trip across was going too slowly. To his dismay the engine gave out when they were only halfway across. For a few minutes the boat drifted in the strong current before the motor was restarted: *"Suddenly the boat bumped alongside a groyne, veered round and a voice croaked, "All right. Let's be having you."* [80]

The boat and its crew went back across the river as soon as the last passenger disembarked. The General and his staff made their way through the mud along the same path that fresh boats were still coming down and was greeted by a familiar face. Lt-Colonel Henniker was glad to see his former commander for it proved that his evacuation plan was showing signs of success. He said, *"I met many old friends: General Urquhart, Eddie Myers and many sappers tramped past in the dark. The plan was work-ing."* [81]

The next stop for the evacuated paratroopers was a tented reception area set up by the 130 Field Ambulance, located behind the winter dyke. Here they were checked for wounds and then escorted in groups to a large barn south of Driel for tea, hot stew, a blanket and rum. The final link in the chain for evacuated members of the British 1st Airborne Division was a ride in a truck to Nijmegen where the sea-borne element of the division was able to clothe them and offer them a place to rest. [82]

However, some had a more difficult crossing. Private D.J. Charlton of R company tells of his experience: *"By 2 am the boats had reduced to six or seven and there was still hundreds of men on or near the river, they were taking 15 or 20 minutes to return and each boat could only take 12 men, so they couldn't possibly move all these before daylight. We had got most of the Padre's walking wounded on to boats, and as I went back for two more, he told me to make this the last, and try to get over myself.*

"I took Donald Rainbridge and Corporal Fred Whiting with me...I managed to get Donald and Fred into a boat, but the engineer manning the boat told me that was enough, but he agreed that I could hang on the side and be dragged over but it was my choice, the boat pulled away with me clinging to the side of it; it was the longest few minutes of my life, it was very cold and the current very strong, it was trying to pry me from the boat, I managed to hang on by changing hands, just as we were nearing the south bank the boat was caught by a burst of machine gun fire. Several men were hit including myself, I felt a burning sensation in my stomach, head, left arm and hand.

"I must have cried out because the engineer at the tiller grabbed my smock collar and kept me afloat until we reached the bank, the boat was full of water and totally useless, the Canadian dragged me onto dry land, as the other fit men did for the wounded the Canadian went off to find a medic. We had drifted downstream some way and it was a while before he came back with help, meanwhile I found that Donald Bainbridge and Fred Whiting had been hit yet again, both in the neck and chest, and in the sunken boat were three Scottish Borderers all dead. As for me, my stomach hurt but the rest were just superficial and were bleeding freely, my head and face were full of wooden splinters from the frame of the canvas boat." [83]

Although Private Charlton makes reference to a canvas boat, it can be assumed that because of the length of time for him to cross (a few minutes) and the fact that he identifies the coxswain as a Canadian his rescuers were from the 23rd. There were only a few recorded instances of men clinging on to the sides of the boats and being dragged across the river, as the speed of the storm boats and the exhaustion of the evacuees prevented them from retaining their grip throughout the crossing. Many of these desperate men were forced to let go and were swept down river, accounting for some of the dead who washed ashore over the following days.

How Many Boats?

As Corporal McLachlan and his crew raced back and forth and new boats were launched, there was still no sign of the second and fourth boats. This worried Lieutenant Cronyn even though some men claimed to have seen Lieutenant Martin in his trench coat on the dyke on the north shore commanding the evacuation from that side. But the crew that was supposed to have delivered him to the north bank hadn't been seen since they had dispatched at 2145 hours. As the other boats started to come back with survivors, there were reports that one of the boats had received a direct mortar hit on the way to the north shore. One man who claimed to have seen this is Private T.W. Pearce of the Glider Pilot Regiment who saw, *"The Germans were firing mortar shells wildly as one felt they didn't know exactly where we were; one shell hit a boat which was half-way across - how many survivors I will never know."* [84] In an effort to set things straight, Lieutenant Cronyn sent his Platoon Sergeant, Sergeant W. G. Willick across in one of the 260th Field Company's, RE Assault boats to try to locate Lt. Martin. He searched up and down the far shore and saw no sign of him or the crew. With this news, Major Tucker and Lieutenant Cronyn were convinced that it and its crew had been lost on their first crossing.

During all of this, Corporal Smith, in charge of the fourth boat, floated back to the south side of the river on his greatcoat. The trapped air held within the thick blanket material was enough for Smith to remain buoyant. On his return, he reported to the beach master, Lieutenant Cronyn, that his boat had capsized when a mortar shell landed close to it, causing everyone in the over-loaded boat to instinctively throw himself away from the blast. All but he and four of his passengers were lost. Included in those killed were both his crew, Sappers Hope and Thompson*. As even more boats were launched a steady stream

* Since most of the men in this boat were wounded and incapable of swimming it would explain why so few of them made it to the south shore. It also explains the disappearance of the 4th boat. It floated down the river headed towards the North Sea, empty of crew and passengers.

Above: Corporal Sidney Smith, taken the day after. His expression says it all. In charge of the 3rd boat, it capsized and he only survived because his great coat had filled with air and kept him afloat until he could reach the shore.
(MacNeil Family)

Norman 'Moose' Caldwell of St. Stephen, New Brunswick. Not the biggest, but widely believed to be the strongest man in the company. After Arnhem, his 'little' brother Elmer joined the company and together with four others they made up the Strong Gang. It took six men to carry a section of Bailey Bridging (600 pounds of steel). In a rush, the group could carry two at a time. (Luuk Buist)

of men were organized into carrying parties, each fighting the mud and the terrain to bring all of the 14 boats to the water. In addition to the large boats, the Evinrude motors and gasoline had to be brought over this route. Every piece of equipment that was needed had to be carried down this path in the dark.

According to the official War Record, a boat was launched approximately every twenty minutes, with the last one entering the water at 0330 hours. This would mean that the fifth boat was launched at 2255 hours, the sixth at 2315 hours and the seventh at 2335 hours. Half of the boats would have been launched in two hours. The other seven would all be in the water by 0155 hours, not 0330 hours if the War Record's account was to be believed. However, as the night wore on, the men became exhausted so the rate of delivery slowed down. Another reason why the 23rd was unable to maintain its initial pace was that 3 boats had to be recovered from the overturned truck. This took time, considering that the truck was at the far end of the orchard. Earlier Lieutenant Kennedy had made sure that all the previous boat lorries had driven as close to the winter dyke as possible in order to cut down the carrying distance for the heavy boats.

Although all 14 Storm boats had been removed from the trucks and launched on the river, they were not all operational at the same time. Of the first four boats launched only one, crewed by Corporal McLachlan, had successfully evacuated soldiers from the north bank. Lieutenant Cronyn estimated that, *"no more than three or four [boats were] in use at one time. All boats were used until damaged by enemy fire or motor shortening due to heavy rain."* [85] The War Diary of the 23rd records that a number of boats had been holed by machine gun fire or had been hit by submerged obstacles. A further cause for the damaged boats was terrain that had damaged the first boat. And although the ground that the boats were carried over had been roughly cleared of debris, more than one boat was damaged on the way down to the river. This may account for some of the damage that the war diary attributes to enemy fire, although other damage was legitimately caused by the Germans before the boats even reached the river.

Lt. Cronyn noted that throughout the night, *"The orchard from which we had started was being heavily shelled. Mortar bombs and machine gun bullets were coming in. Tracers raced in, caroming (sic) off the gronyn (sic) by the river. Bullets seemed to go in and through the boats and between our legs and arms, but by some miracle, none of us was hit. Boats were crashing on obstacles as they came into shore and some were holed so badly that they had to be abandoned. The shelling and mortaring subsided somewhat after midnight but we were never free of them."* [86]

It was both fortunate that the 23rd Field Company, RCE had taken as many boats as it did for the evacuation, to replace those boats damaged in the night, and regrettable that they were unable to take any more Storm boats which were proving to be so useful during the operation.

On Through the Night

In time, the boats constantly racing back and forth across the river began to run low on fuel. Sergeant King and Sapper Victor Titus were one of the two teams assigned the task of refueling the boats. Sergeant King estimated that he refueled a boat an hour on average at his station 100 yards up from the launching area. This in itself was no easy task as the refueling site along the riverbank was exposed to repeated enemy fire. Sergeant King described the scene: *"Jerry would send up a flare then the water was just boiling with machine gun fire. 88's would burst in the air. The Germans fired flares into the air that made it seem like daylight. Every time a flare went up, we dove under the water. The river was boiling, just boiling!"* [87] This made the refueling a very risky and time consuming affair, with the threat of fire or explosion just a hot piece of shrapnel away. And fuel was spilled along the path. One of those assigned to carry fuel for the boats was Sapper Willie Richardson. In his opinion: *"We spilled so much that I think we lost more than we brought forward."* [87] Boats used to continue the evacuation efforts, while refueling was going on, came from the company's reserve. George King was also in charge of the reserve and he stated, *"Five boats were kept in reserve and one by one they replaced damaged boats."* [88]

The major flaw with the Storm boats was discovered by the company during the night. As stated earlier, the Evinrude engines were originally designed for the commercial market and were susceptible to moisture entering the engines. On previous operations such as the Seine River crossing and pre-invasion exercises in Britain, this fault was not apparent, as they had been conducted during clear, dry weather. However, the constant downpour that night drenched everything, including the spark plugs and electrical circuits in the engines. Added to this were the frantic efforts by the boat crews to avoid German fire and beach their crafts at speed when landing. The result was a backwash of water that engulfed the engines. As a result the Storm boats frequently had to be taken out of service to have their engines replaced and attempts were made to dry out the electrical components. This was done in a small hole in the riverbank that Sapper Earl Fisher of the E and M platoon called, 'the Shop'.[89] Each of the motors had to be dismantled from the boats and carried to, 'the Shop'. A pan of burning gas was used to dry out the spark plugs. Afterwards, both Sapper Fisher and Lance Corporal Arthur Gamble would attempt to start the dried out engine. Success usually included a moment of flame escaping from the exhaust, followed by both men jumping back into, 'the Shop' since the flame routinely drew enemy fire onto their position. The six members of the 10th Field Park Company, RCE were kept busy all night trying to keep the Storm boats supplied with working motors. This was an uphill battle as the rain increased in intensity.

The 3rd Canadian Electrical and Mechanical Platoon's (a detachable part of the 10th Field Park Company, RCE) War Diary states: *"When all boats had passed through them, over the flood walls and to the beaches, they mixed more fuel, gathered up what spare parts they thought would be necessary and proceeded to a new position at the beach. Here they gathered all spare engines around them. During the operations, when an engine failed, the boat crew came to this position, took a spare engine away and told the Mtce. Sec [Maintenance Section] where the broken engine was. The fitters then fixed the broken engine on the spot and it became another spare. In all they fixed 8 to 10 engines. The chief trouble was wet spark plugs which they removed, dried and replaced, or replaced with new plugs. They were kept very busy all night."*[90]

All the maintenance work necessary to repair the engines prevented the Storm boats from all operating at the same time.

Meanwhile, boats see-sawed back and forth doing the best that they could. Men struggled to carry the boats through the mud and wet grass down to the river. Other men struggled to cross the swift and wide river to pick up and bring back as many survivors as possible and even still more men struggled to patch up the holed boats and help with the wounded. All this happened while under heavy fire from German positions on the north bank. The reason for all these selfless acts are best summed up by what an unidentified Canadian engineer told Lieutenant Williams of the 1st Battalion, the Parachute Regiment: *"We are mighty proud to take you fellows across."* [91]

The greatest risk for the boat crews was the engine quitting during mid-crossing. This was when the boats were at their most vulnerable to the constant German fire skimming across the water from the north shore. The engineers were either forced to slowly paddle towards the south bank or remain bobbing in the river like sitting ducks, attempting to restart their engine. In most boats paddling wasn't possible because there weren't enough paddles and their passengers were in no physical state to assist. In one instance when the outboard motor couldn't be restarted, the crew asked all soldiers with rifles to start paddling. This they all did, except for the man in front of Private Arthur Shearwood, of the 11th Battalion, The Parachute Regiment. Shearwood tapped the man in front of him and told him to start paddling. The man looked at him without expression and said while pointing to his bandaged shoulder, *"I can't I've lost an arm."* [92] Most crews, however, had faith in their engines and were determined to re-start them. This faith, coupled with liberal blasphemies, were able to resurrect most of the engines. Major Alan Bush of the 3rd Battalion, The Parachute Regiment found himself in exactly that situation when the engine on the Storm boat evacuating him suddenly cut out: *"I thought I had heard every oath in the English language but I heard a few new ones from those Canadians until they got it going again."* [93] The other risk that Storm boats stalled in mid-river faced was being swamped by the wake of another Storm boat. Although there were no recorded instances of this happening, the 260th Field Company, RE's War Diary does state that the passing of the larger Storm boats had overturned several of their assault boats. This was one of the dangers that Lieutenant-Colonel Henniker wanted to avoid when he planned this operation. However, in the chaos of the darkness, boat crews didn't really know exactly where they were or what was directly in front of them.

This made it all the more amazing that the Storm boat crews were able to spot lone paratroopers trying to swim across the river and drag them into their boats. An attempt to swim the river was made by Sergeant Alfred Roullier, of the 1st Airlanding Brigade's artillery. Just as he began to feel as if his attempt was failing, a boat came along beside him and someone grabbed his collar to keep the struggling sergeant afloat. Roullier heard a voice encouraging him. *"It's okay mate. Keep going. Keep going."* But Rouliier's strength was giving out and he was sure he would drown. Then he heard the same voice again, *"bloody good, old boy,"* and a Canadian engineer lifted him into the boat. The dazed sergeant was only able to ask, *"Where the hell am I?"* to which the Canadian grinned and told him, *"You're almost home."* [94] However, being plucked out of the river by a passing Storm boat sometimes had unforeseen consequences, as Signalman James Cockrill discovered. As Cockrill was making his attempt to swim to freedom, he heard a Canadian voice say, *"All right, buddy, don't worry. I've got you."* After he was hauled onboard, he felt the boat lurch as it touched the shore and had the shock of his night. *"I nearly cried when I found I was back where I started,"* because the boat had been on it way to the north bank to pick up another load of paratroopers. Even though the boat was overloaded and German machine gun fire pursued it, Corkrill's second attempt to cross the Neder Rijn was more successful than his first.[95]

There were cases where the engine quit on the north bank, which at least allowed for the possibility of being towed back by another boat. This increased the risk for both boats as it necessitated a very slow crossing. The maneuver had to be undertaken at slow speed so the second boat did not take on water and sink. The crew of the tow boat had to constantly monitor the condition of the boat behind it to prevent this from happening: an almost impossible task in the pitch black of the night. Around 02:00, Private John Crosson of No. 6 platoon, B coy, 7th KOSB described the situation: *"The motor had stopped and the Sapper was trying to restart it with a cord. Another boat came alongside to load up. Our Sapper persuaded its pilot to give us a tow across. This was very slow progress, against a swift river it seemed like ages before a bump was felt as both boats arrived on the south bank."* [96]

A new crew replaced Corporal McLachlan's after his fifteenth trip across. He and his crew had brought back roughly 210 men; this was approximately one-tenth of the total number of men that the 23rd Field Company, RCE brought back in 150 trips that night. Sapper Raymond Lebouthillier of Gaspe, Quebec was the boatman on 26 trips that collected well over 500 men. After his first fourteen trips with his first crew, he refused to quit and joined a fresh crew for another twelve trips. He took part in approximately one-sixth of the total trips that the company made that night. Lebouthillier spent five hours going back and forth across the river, jumping into the cold water each time they came to shore to prevent the Storm boat from being damaged on the rocks. This was necessary as the crew dared not shut the engine off for fear it would not restart and because the engines had no reverse to slow the boat's approach. He only stopped in his efforts when he was finally ordered to the company's rest area in a state of exhaustion. Major Tucker was so impressed with his exemplary performance that he was recommended for the Military Medal.

The 4th Parachute Squadron, RE reached the river between 2215 to 2230 hrs and all sixty-four members were across by 0030. Captain J. Smith of the 4th Parachute Squadron, RE said, *"When we eventually got to the river I took my Troop a couple of hundred yards upstream and stopped on one of the stone groins that stuck out into the river and began flashing my small flashlight at the south bank. We were getting very discouraged when we had no response for what seemed like hours and we were trying to figure out whether one of us could swim the river and convince whoever was on the other side that we were not Germans. I was a fairly good swimmer but I was cold, wet and tired and it all just looked to be too much. Eventually a boat came chugging towards us, a Canadian Sapper had decided to take a chance but by the time he arrived our numbers had increased to about double so he had to make four trips loaded to the gunnels to get us all across. Each time he did come back for more which took a lot of guts consider-*

ing what was going on." [97] The boatman in question may have
been Sapper Raymond Lebouthillier. When Major Tucker described Sapper Lebouthillier's actions in his recommendation for
a Military Medal it corresponds closely with the account Captain
Smith gave of his rescue. In part, the recommendation by Major
Tucker stated, *"Regardless of personal danger, he directed his
craft well out to the flanks of the bridgehead calling out for survivors of the airborne troops, who could not make their way to organized embarkation beaches, to make themselves known, so that
they might be taken off. On every crossing he jumped into the water as the boat was coming ashore to hold it off from crashing
onto a rock or any other obstacle which might crash the hull and
sink the craft."* [98] For these actions Sapper Lebouthillier received
one of two Military Medals awarded to the 23rd that night.

Captain Brown of the 4th Parachute Squadron, RE and some
of his men found an abandoned Assault boat and took fourteen
trips across the river. His plan was to return with three men to
pick up another load of men. However, when they reached the
south shore, they were greeted by what he describes as an enor-
mous Canadian Engineer Officer who had other ideas. When the
Captain started back to the boat 6'-4" Lieutenant Bob Tate put
his large hand on the Captain's shoulder and asked him, *"Where
the hell are you going?"* [98a] The Captain told him of the plan to go
back for the rest of his men and was told by Lieutenant Tate that
there were well rested sappers who would do the job.

Besides men coming back in the boats, news filtered over
from the north shore. The carrying parties, which delivered the
boats to the launch site, had to walk back along the same path as
the people that had just been rescued, so they were able to pick
up quite a bit of information about the situation. They relayed it
back to people like Lieutenant Kennedy. This is how the Lieutenant - who was still running up and down the route, supervising
the transfer of the boats - heard a report that the second boat
had received a direct mortar hit and that all hands were lost.
Even though he didn't see him go, he knew that his friend, Lieutenant Martin - the man who he joined up with several years
earlier - was on one of the boats that didn't come back.

It was turning out to be a very rough night for him. His driver Sapper "Buck" McKee, whose primary job was to keep the jeep ready in case it was needed, was wounded in the orchard by shelling and was sent back as a serious casualty where he later succumbed to his wounds. Another member of the recce party, Sgt. Don Barnes was also hit by shellfire during the night. He was on loan to Major Tucker because Lieutenant Kennedy didn't need him and he said, *"the Major was always short of help. So I had loaned him Don for the night."* [99] Lt. Kennedy was told that his beloved Sergeant would probably not make it because he took a big piece of shrapnel in the head. However, they rushed him to the hospital at Driel anyway to do what they could for him. Other casualties occurred when a mortar bomb landed near the command post - located on the beach - and a piece of shrapnel hit Sapper J.P. Letoqueux. The shelling also seriously wounded Sapper D.E. Francis.

Above: a sapper of the 23rd Field Company, RCE at the controls of a Storm Boat with a boatload of soldiers from the 101st Airborne Division. This photo was taken at Nijmegen in November 1944 as the airborne division was being relieved of its duties on The Island.

The Last Boats

By 0330 hours the last boat was in the water and Corporal Robinson - who had been helping to carry the boats all night - was in command. He and his crew left to complete the first of six journeys across the river. At the same time Lieutenant John Stevenson of the 1st Reconnaissance Squadron describes one of the recurring themes of the night when rain and engines are mixed: *"When we got into the boat, the Canadian Engineer pulled at the lanyard to start the outboard motor, but nothing happened. I remember we were stuck there at half-past three in the morning, wondering if we'd still be there when daylight came. All the time he was pulling away he kept saying, `The bastard-the bastard-the bastard, when suddenly it `phutt-phutted' into life and we were away and off to the opposite bank."* 100

Stevenson's experience also illustrates another underlying theme of the night; that determination and perseverance, along with the generous use of profanities, allowed the Canadian engineers of the 23rd to accomplish the enormity of their task.

With the last Storm boat delivered to the launching site, Lieutenant Kennedy's duties were complete and Major Tucker no longer needed him. With nothing to do, he asked permission to look along the shoreline for a usable boat and found a canvas Assault boat. When he proposed to assist in the evacuation with it, Major Tucker denied the request as he thought that the current was too strong. So Lieutenant Kennedy went searching again. The 260th Field Company, RE War Diary supports Major Tucker's assessment. It states: *"As wind and current increase crews had to be increased from 4 to 6 men thus reducing capacity. Storm boats getting into stride by now and doing good work. By 0500 hours assault boats become practically unmanageable. Men very tired and strong tide."* 101 Lt-Colonel Henniker comments on the dwindling effectiveness of the assault boats: *"...it became almost impossible to maneuver them at all. I had to stop them, though the storm boats with their horsepower could still reap a fair return."* 102 This placed the burden of further evacuation squarely on the shoulders of the 23rd Field Company, RCE.

Some of the boats whose engines failed midstream were caught by the strong current and floated downstream, out of the reach of the temporary workshop. These boats had to be abandoned as the crews struggled to make it back to the company. It was one of these boats that Lieutenant Kennedy found after he *"went stumbling around in the dark"* looking for a boat that could handle the current. *"Managed to get the motor started, but we didn't try to handle these cranky heavy boats without at least 2 men, so I left it and went back to Mike* (Major Tucker). *He sent L/ Cpl. A.D. Gillis and Sapper David John McCready with me to do what we could. I'd guess that it was between 4:30 and 5:00 am by the time we had checked out the boat and started across."* [103]

Sapper McCready was the first to volunteer, which was becoming increasingly dangerous with the coming of the dawn.

With Corporal Gillis operating the motor, they crossed the river and followed the shore downstream until they found a mass of Airborne troops waiting to be evacuated. Lieutenant Kennedy describes the almost comical event when he reached the desperate men still trapped on the northern bank, as dawn approached: *"Gillis operating the motor put the bow up to the shore and I started to direct the embarkation. I found myself being pushed backwards by an uncontrollable mass of men. Made the futile gesture of drawing my Browning, then realized 1) the paratroopers couldn't see it: 2) no way I'd fire at the men we came to rescue; and 3) best not to attract attention in what was really enemy territory. I put the gun back in the holster and went down with the ship - in four feet of cold water."* [104]

Lieutenant S. Relidzinski of the Polish Parachute Brigade witnessed the sinking of this boat: *"In the breaking daylight only a handful of boats were still ferrying. The men became dazed, frustrated and panicky. One of the boats ready to start taking a new load across was suddenly mobbed by the unruly crowd and sunk in the shallow waters. A young British officer* shouted: Sol-*

---

* = The British officer might have been the CO of the 260th Field Company, RE, Major Tony Vinycomb, the CO of the 260th Field Company, R.E. who Lieutenant-Colonel Henniker said was an accomplished waterman and that he had made several journeys across the river in his company's Assault boats.

diers, you are British, behave like gentlemen.' The crowd calmed down and some men started undressing ready to swim." [105]

The water in Kennedy's boat had to be bailed out, a tough task for tired men on a steep and slippery bank. The difficulty of this chore allowed Lieutenant Kennedy to reestablish some semblance of discipline while loading the boat. However, the all too predictable result of submerging the motor in water meant that the boat would have to be paddled back across to the south bank. Lieutenant Kennedy ordered the passengers and crew to use all available rifles to paddle the boat to safety. The strong current affected the crossing, pushing them downstream. When they finally made it to the south bank, the rain had stopped. They had landed at the 260th Field Company, RE operating site.

As Lt. Kennedy watched his passengers disappear in the predawn grayness heading south to safety, his crew spotted another abandoned Storm boat, as well as an abandoned Assault boat stuck on the next groin upstream. An attempt was made to start the newly discovered Evinrude engine. After many pulls on the flywheel and much verbal encouragement, the engine roared into life. Since the darkness needed to evacuate the men was rapidly disappearing, the three men agreed to attempt to re-cross the river with the functioning Storm boat towing the two boats behind it. As Lieutenant Kennedy remembered, *"Gillis and McCready agreed to try to use all three craft. We tied them stern to bow, pushed out into the little bay between groynes and the boys paddled to keep straightened out and lines away from the propeller while I fought with the motor. When it caught, we seemed to be back up river and across in no time. The light was better, the paratroopers were organized in lines and we loaded all three boats and pushed off again. The motor roared and we brought the three boatloads safely to the south shore."* [106]

Dawn

When dawn broke, Major Tucker thought that he had only 2 boats left. The reserve was empty of functioning boats. Sergeant George King said: *"Lieutenant Cronyn ordered me to take out the last boat, but try as I could I couldn't get it started."* [107]

Lt-Colonel Henniker stated how he saw things: *"When dawn broke, things went less smoothly there was no longer any flash to reveal where the enemy lay and fired from, and they became more daring. The boats on the river were now, clearly visible and each trip a hazardous journey. Little fountains of water marked where German mortar bombs had fallen and the struggles of men in the water brought rescue boats to pull them out. This clearly could not be allowed to go on much longer."* [108] The flashes from German fire had allowed the 43rd Wessex Division on the south bank to locate and suppress the German's fire. It was 0545 hours when Henniker made the decision to call a halt to Operation Berlin.

The 43rd Division's artillery started laying down a smoke screen in an effort to cover the boats from the enemy. Lt-Colonel Henniker said that it worked until, *"a morning breeze sprang up,"* [109] *and* then it had very little effect covering the view of the river. Lieutenant Cronyn thought that the guns ran out of smoke shells. For local concealment the engineers were given smoke canisters which were equally ineffective. Lieutenant Cronyn describes that, *"It was somewhat like trying to hide a cup of coffee with the smoke from one cigarette."* [110]

Lieutenant Kennedy and Sapper McCready, knowing that men were still left on the north bank waiting to be rescued, set out to try their luck again. Lance Corporal Gillis decided not to go back in what looked like a suicide mission because he had a wife and a child back in Canada to think about. Using the two Storm boats, one towing the other, the two engineers set out with little darkness left to obscure them from the German gunners. On arriving on the north bank it was clear there was no way that these boats could take all the desperate men waiting to be evacuated. All traces of the cloak of night had gone and this was clearly the last ticket out of an increasingly dangerous spot. One of those who would be left behind was Private John "Tex" Ranger of 20th Platoon of D company, 1st Battalion, The Border Regiment: *"On the night of the withdrawal across the river, we must have been some of the last to go down, on arrival at the river, there were about 100 people waiting for the boats, we were there only a short time when we heard a chap say, 'Sorry this is our last run, we will not be returning. Just before there was a shot and someone shouted, "if you try to rush the boats, I will use this on you." I think one or two were panicking."* [111]

The Airborne troops overloaded the boats and Lt. Kennedy couldn't pull the starting rope of the Evinrude motor. Men had to lean out over the water so the Lieutenant had room to pull the rope. It didn't start. Some of the thirty-six men that had managed to cram into the boat wanted to use their rifles to paddle across, but the Lieutenant vetoed the idea. He noticed that German machine guns on the hills were raking the river again. At the moment they were relatively safe inside of the groins. He tried the motor again and again.

Fed up with waiting, the men in the second boat cut its line and paddled off against the Lieutenant's protest. All discipline had broken down. McCready was in that boat, but he was outnumbered, so his protests were also ignored. Unfortunately, the machine guns got a clear shot at the slow moving target. Only nine of the twenty-five passengers made it to the south bank. Of them, four were killed before they made it over the dyke to safety. McCready was wounded, getting nicked by a bullet, as he climbed over the dyke. He went straight to the aid station to get patched up before he reported back for duty. For his perseverance and actions throughout the night, Major Tucker nominated Sapper McCready for the Military Medal; his was to be the second one earned by the 23rd during Operation Berlin.

Seeing what happened to McCready's boat was too much for some people. One of them was Lieutenant Kennedy, who refuses to talk about it. Another was Lt-Colonel Henniker who witnessed the slaughter of McCready's boat and thought that it was the young Canadian officer that was piloting the boat. What he didn't realize was that Lieutenant Kennedy was still on the wrong side of the river, trying to get the motor started as the tired passengers watched helplessly. So as the guns stopped and the RE were putting their boats back into the trucks, the last boat was on its own.

Craftsman Ted Sullivan of No. 6 LAD (1st Airborne RCEME) was one of those men in the boat: *"By now it was getting light. I think I must have got the last boat to make it across and it nearly didn't. It was manned by a Canadian engineer and, for a nerve-racking few minutes, he had a devil of a job starting it up. Eventually, he got the motor going and we were on our way. Sometimes, when I happen to be sitting alone in the corner of my local pub, settling nicely into my third pint, I think 'Did I really do and see all those things? Was I really there? Perhaps I saw it on the television."* [113]

With the motor finally started, they moved cautiously into the river. Lieutenant Kennedy tells what happened next: *"The blunt bow of the storm boat was so close to the water that I didn't dare use much power for fear of catching a ripple and driving her under. The machine guns were still firing, the bullets making interesting patterns on the water around us, but they never actually got onto us. A single projectile hit the man who was jammed under my right elbow, with a sound like the blow of a club. He jerked once and never moved again. The bow of the boat hit the beach and 10 seconds later the dead paratrooper and I were alone. It was 7:20 a.m. and full light on Tuesday the 26th, the ninth day after Market Garden was launched with such high hopes."* [114]

This was the last trip of the night. No more boats on the river! With the river in clear view of the German gunners, any more trips would be suicidal.

It was over.

After Effects

On the north side of the river, SS Hauptsturmfuher Muller recorded what happened next: *"But then it stopped - all of a sudden - the silence appeared treacherous to all and almost 'hurt'. Was it all over? Would it start again? The Red Devils had withdrawn and disappeared during the night behind the curtain of dirt and destruction."* [115]

During the operation Major Tucker tried to record the number of men being delivered, but the rain had turned the paper in his hands to pulp. He quickly gave up the idea of writing anything down, so an actual account of how many men the 23rd Field Company, RCE ferried across that night remains uncertain. The official tally of how many men were evacuated across the river is 2398, although current research into the battle has recognized that 2406 men escaped the cauldron on the north bank during the night of 25/26 September. The 23rd Field Company, RCE, in 150 trips, evacuated the majority; approximately 2000 men. However, this figure could be much higher, possibly 2500; especially if the individual unit's totals of men evacuated is added together and miscellaneous personnel are factored in - such as shot down RAF aircrews; even a German prisoner and a Dutch guide were taken across that night.

Over two thousand men who had held the perimeter at Oosterbeek crossed the Neder Rijn during the night. They were all cold, wet and exhausted and many were happy just to be out of the hell of their nine-day ordeal. Each man who survived had a story about his particular rescue. The story that the free world would hear broadcast on 28 September came from Stanley Maxted. A Canadian reporter, Maxted landed with the 1st Airborne Division on the first day to document its victory. After making reports throughout the battle, he was evacuated during Operation Berlin and a record of his account was originally broadcast on the BBC shortly after the evacuation. Part of his broadcast was: *"At the river we lie motionless – some for hours – until the time comes to scramble over the dykes and into the banks while the 2ⁿᵈ Army guns thunder their anger on the enemy positions. We drag ourselves into a boat. Just now I heard a voice that was shear music saying, You better step lively boys. It t'aint healthy around here. It was a Canadian voice and these are Canadian Engineers who are manning the assault craft who hauled them over land under enemy fire through a narrow German flanked corridor, over fields and dykes to come and get us out of hell across this swift flowing river."* [116]

This is how most civilians found out that Operation Market Garden had ended, and not in success.

Unbeknownst to anyone a teddy bear belonging to Commander Wolters, a member of the Dutch SAS team that had landed with the British 1ˢᵗ Airborne Division, was successfully evacuated. It was supposed to have been a present for his daughter who lived in Nazi occupied Holland. If the plan had been successful he would have presented it to her. Sadly, he clutched the teddy bear as he crossed. [117] The bear would have to wait until spring when Wolters could give it to her. This was a fitting symbol to illustrate the failure of Operation Market Garden - the would-be liberators sadly leaving the helpless behind.

Many Airborne soldiers, too, were left behind on the north side. Some tried to swim or use the life preservers that had been brought over while others were just too tired to try. The British 1ˢᵗ Airborne Division's estimate is that three hundred men were left behind on the north bank while men who were there believed it was smaller, approximately a hundred to a hundred and fifty. Most of the men belonged to one of two units: The Borders or the South Staffordshire Regiments. They were the last to leave their positions on the perimeter and the last to have any chance to find a spot on the boats.

Now was time to mourn the dead, treat the wounded and hope that the missing would show up. Some did. Many crews who had been carried downstream when the motors of their boats failed had worked their way back to safety along the shore. Lieutenant John Cronyn was instructed to stay behind and wait for any stragglers as the rest of the 23ʳᵈ left to return to its advanced rendezvous at Valburg. He was delighted to see Lieutenant Kennedy come over the winter dyke: *"He was absolutely ashen and terribly shaken up by that last trip across, made under heavy machine gun fire and with very heavy casualties. He certainly deserved the Military Cross, which he received for his performance that night. It had been a terrifying experience for all involved, one they would not soon forget."* [118]

Lieutenant John Cronyn knew that boat numbers 2 and 4 failed to return and that several witnesses reported seeing that the second boat had received a direct mortar hit and sunk. However, since it was dark, the witnesses weren't completely confident in this. He hoped that they were wrong: *"By this time the sun was coming up and things were relatively quiet. I had been talking to a British soldier* [most likely from the 130th Brigade of the 43rd Division] *in a slit trench after getting Russ Kennedy off to Nijmegen and had just walked away from him when a mortar dropped right on top of him, wounding him severely. The Red Cross unit that picked him up agreed to send an ambulance under a Red Cross flag down to the ferry site to look around for wounded and Sergeant W.G. Willick and I set out downstream, walking behind the winter dyke, to see if we could locate any of our missing personnel. We found a number of wounded paratroopers who had swum the river and then been shot in attempting to get over the winter dyke. They were hiding in Dutch summer homes built into the side of the dyke. None of our missing were found by either party."* [119]

Unfortunately, none of the missing six men showed up and Lieutenant John Cronyn waited in vain. With very little chance of anyone showing up during daylight, he left at 1030 hours. He hoped that maybe they would show up when it got dark.

For the rest of the 23rd, breakfast was waiting for them at Valburg Station. Fortunately, many of the crews that had lost power midstream managed to beach their boats on the right side of the river and found their way back to Valburg. At breakfast, stories were exchanged as more and more crews found their way home and slowly events of the night were pieced together. It had been a long difficult night. Many problems had been overcome and the British 1st Airborne Division had been evacuated from its nine day siege; although bedraggled and battle-weary.

No matter the true figure of how many men were evacuated, the 23rd Field Company, RCE shone. They succeeded in taking on a difficult and dirty task and performed it well. However, there was a price to pay. As time passed bodies were found downstream and identified. It became clear that of the missing six men, five had indeed sacrificed their lives that night. A total of seven men of the company died that night, six who were boat crew and Sapper McKee* on shore, as well as four who were wounded. Even though everyone thought otherwise, Sergeant Don Barnes survived, was sent back to England and to quote Russ Kennedy, *"he lived to a respectable age with a plate in his forehead."* [120]

In addition to the two Military Medals won by Sappers McCready and Lebouthillier of the 23rd, Lieutenant Kennedy was awarded the Military Cross *"For conspicuous gallantry and devotion to duty during operations in the Nijmegen 'Island'."* [121] The Lieutenant's decoration was awarded well after Operation Berlin and encompassed the gallantry he showed in a later operation, Operation Pegasus 2. The fourth member of the unit to be recognized in part for the role he played during Operation Berlin was Major Tucker, who was given the Distinguished Service Order.

---

* = Sapper Buck Mckee died shortly after he reached the hospital in Driel. He is buried in the Oosterbeek War Cemetery. L.J. Roherty has never been found and to this day still has no known grave. The only hint of what happened to him can be found in The History of the Corps of Royal Canadian Engineering Volume 2, where it reports that one of the men died as a prisoner of war. But neither he - nor the others - is listed in any POW records. Is it possible that he survived the mortar attack and had washed ashore only to be captured by the Germans and died while enroute to the hospital? No one knows. However, when he was missing he was still being paid by the army and the payment only stopped when his body was found downstream with a Polish paratrooper. I believe that he died on the 25th from a direct hit by a mortar bomb and that no one wanted to try to collect the overpayment from his relatives so they just list him as 'died whilst POW' instead.

After Arnhem

On the morning of September 26th, after breakfast in Valburg, a very tired group of men were trucked back to Nijmegen to rejoin the rest of the company. On the 28th they were billeted in Bourg-Leopold where they stayed under the control of the British XXX Corps until the end of the month. During that time, a letter was received from the Chief Engineer of the Corps. It read: *"On the departure of Canadian Army Troops Engineers from 30th Corps, I should like to thank you and them for their excellent and very courageous work with Storm boats in the evacuation from Arnhem. The work they did was carried out under very difficult and dangerous conditions of enemy fire and weather, but was exceedingly efficiently done, and was instrumental in the safe return of a very large proportion of the Airborne troops."* [122]

On October 4th Sapper David L.G. Hope's body was recovered from the Rhine near Remmerden. A week later, L/Cpl. Ryan was also pulled from the river. Lieutenant Martin, Sapper Thompson and Sapper Magnusson were also recovered from the river during this time. Only Sapper Leslie J. Roherty's body was never found.

Once back with the Canadian 1st Army, they were put to work chopping wood. Major Tucker put his tongue in his cheek and wrote this entry: *"Our Victory Loan Campaign does well, and the objectives is exceeded by $1,500.00."* [123]

He and his men felt that they were meant for better things and that their current job of cutting wood was beneath them. Maybe they were right because it was during this time that they developed a means of water-proofing the Evinrude motors and had worked out the arrangements whereby Storm boats could be carried with metal bars. An experiment by the 5th Field Company, RCE proved these recommendations to be beneficial.

The 23rd Field Company, RCE built a bridge over the Albert Canal and named it the Martin Bridge after their fallen officer, Lt. James Russell Martin. This was the second time since coming to the European mainland in July that the 23rd Field Company,

RCE honoured one of their fallen officers by naming a bridge after him, much in the same way a bridge in France was named after Captain J. Reynolds. The Martin Bridge was used by the locals for the next forty years until it was replaced.

In November, they were recruited for the Pegasus II operation, which entailed rescuing British Airborne soldiers who had evaded capture and remained at large on the north side of the Lower Rhine. A few weeks earlier, Pegasus I had been very successful, even though the British sappers with their Assault boats had to cross the river three times to get all of the evaders out of German held territory. It was decided to use Storm boats for the next one, so the 23rd were called.

Unfortunately, due to the publicity of the success of Pegasus I, the Germans had more troops in the area and were on the lookout for another attempt. In spite of the efforts of the men of the 23rd and the American paratroopers, only seven men made it safely back to Allied lines. The problem was the increased German vigilance on the north side of the river.

In December, the 23rd were given the task of training other engineers in the operation of Storm boats. They did this in Nijmegen while temporarily holding the front-line. Fortunately, the Germans didn't know that there weren't any infantry in the area. The training went so well that in the new year two officers and fifteen men were permanently assigned to test new boats and to train agents on how to use them. The rest of the company moved on to work on roads.

On April 12th 1945, the 23rd did what they wanted to do back in September; which was to participate in an assault river crossing. This happened just east of Arnhem at Westervoort and once again their passengers were British, this time from the 49th Division. This unit, under 1st Canadian Army command, finally captured Arnhem.

On the last day of September 1945, the 23rd was disbanded, four days before the rest of ICAT, RCE was dissolved. The tradition of the 23rd Field Company, RCE lives on in the 23rd Field Squadron. They are stationed in Petawawa and every year they hold a "Neder Rijn Celebration".

The Battlefield Today

In 1989, a monument was erected to honour all of the engineers who took part. Proudly, it stands and explains what happened here on a very wet and miserable night in 1944.

Sappers Moose Caldwell, Sandy Morris, Stan Goodall and Clayton Moss represented the 23rd at the opening ceremony. A noted speaker at this event was the celebrated CO of the 2nd Battalion, The Parachute Regiment, John Frost .

The area that the 23rd Field Company, RCE operated in has changed drastically over the years. The apple orchard is gone and is now a field. The river has been totally reworked at some spots and it is impossible to locate the exact launching site. Even the veterans of the 23rd who were at the 50th anniversary couldn't pin-point the precise location. However, they all agreed that the monument is located within the operating site.

After the battle the Allies pulled back from the river and in an effort to flood them out, the Germans blasted the winter dyke, allowing the river to flood the orchard beyond.

When the Germans left, the road was filled in with sand from an area just west of the house in the 23rd area. That area is now a pond which is clearly visible from the road on top of the winter dyke.

The winter dyke has been reworked as well. Its slopes are not as steep as they were in 1944. Yet, there is a place down the road where the slope was just like it was during the war. The slope couldn't be changed at this point because the existing house and barn were too close to the dyke. Even though the slopes of the winter dyke have been elongated, its height is still basically the same. This could not be said for the summer dyke. Erosion and the reworking of the shoreline has reduced its height considerably. Still, even with all of those changes, it is possible to picture the difficulties that all of the engineers had that night. From the area of the monument, the heights of Westerbouwing to the West are dominating and the railroad bridge to the east is all too close. These represent the German positions on the night of the September 25th 1944.

Across the river, very little has changed. The 1000 year old church is a little smaller, but still stands. The path and the little bridge that most of the Airborne troops came down are still in use.

Top Left: the engineer's monument in 2004. (Laura Sliz)

Top right: Harold Cornell, George Willick, Donald Somerville and Don Barnes. (Donald Somerville)

Bottom: the boys in Oosterbeek in 1994. L to r: Cornell, Stan Jr. Goodall, Bob Tate, Donald Somerville, Smoky Latour, Rolly Zinc, Willie Richardson, Unknown, Unknown, George King, Clayton Moss and George Wilson. (George and Ethel King)

Afterward

Until now, in the accounts of Operation Market Garden only a few paragraphs have been dedicated to the evacuation and even fewer of them bother to mention the units involved or how they got there.

This is understandable, such was the confusion of that night, that even those who were there and had been rescued never knew who their saviours were. Due to the confusion many myths have grown around the events of that night. One of these involves the idea that Lieutenant Kennedy brought life belts on his last trip across the river for any one who wouldn't fit on his boat and were willing to attempt to swim the river. Someone, upon reaching the north bank, had in fact left about a hundred life-belts for those who wanted to swim across. It is not certain who left them, possibly Major Vinycomb, of the 260th on his last trip. It is true, however, that the German made lifebelts were found in a supply depot in Nijmegen. However, Lieutenant Kennedy had nothing to do with them being deposited on the north bank. Yet, he has in many books been credited with doing so.

While preparing this book I had the privilege of passing on a few messages from members of the 1st Airborne Division to the men of the 23rd Field Company, R.C.E. One was from M. Potter of the 261st Field Park, RE who said, "*I cannot speak too highly of the bravery and commitment of the Royal Canadian Engineers whose courage helped so many of our forces to escape capture.*"125

Of the four engineer companies, the 20th Field Company, RCE probably had the most frustrating job. Together with the 553rd Field Company, RE they were the victims of bad planning and/or poor communications. At least the RE's Assault boats managed to rescue some men. However, if both of these units weren't set up directly in front of the enemy and stationed east of the Driel Ferry, they would have reaped a much higher return. Again, this had nothing to do with their efforts, for they were more than willing and prepared to do the job.

Even though the 260th Field Company, RE was in a good position, it too was a victim. This time tradition, and the reluctance not to use new technology, forced them to paddle their boats back and forth across the river until the current became too strong and the men too weary to continue. Even so, the support from the Dorsets' sapper platoon couldn't do the impossible. Yet, under the circumstances, they reaped a good return and should be proud of their efforts.

Fortunately, the 23rd Field Company, RCE had the right equipment, was in the right position and had the training and experience to do their job. The fact that all the fatalities in the engineering companies were men of the 23rd proves just how involved they were. All night and into the morning they applied their craft, evacuating the lion's share of 2406 men from a tight noose. Sapper N.C. `Moose' Caldwell was on a boat that crossed countless times. How many times? `*I have no idea,' he said. `I really don't. Over and back, over and back, across the river. No I wasn't scared. I was terrified, terrified."* [126] In a 1994 interview for a Dutch newspaper he said that he still had nightmares about the night of September 25th/26st 1944. This small group of Canadians were sent to the tip of the Allied advance and made a difference.

Appendices

Appendix #1:

The Officers and Men of the 23rd RCE
Who Took Part in Operation Berlin

According to the *Maple Leaf* newspaper, the following men took place in Operation Berlin. The author, Captain Jack Golding, received a list from Major Tucker. However, Captain McIntyre whose name is included doesn't belong on this list because every record states that he was put in charge of the personnel left in Nijmegen. The seventh officer in the 23rd at the time was Lt. Charley Aspler's name who was left in Valburg. It is obvious that the list is incomplete.

Not counting Captain McIntyre there are 4 officers and 46 men. Because the *Maple Leaf* article was published during the war, the casualties have been omitted. They are: Lt. Martin, Cpl. Ryan, Sappers Magnusson, Roherty, Hope, Thompson, McKee, Black, Francis and LeToqueux, who were obviously there.

The total would be 5 officers and 55 men.

According to L/Sgt. George King, the following men were also present: Sgt. Gillard, L/Sgt. Strong and Sappers Victor Titus, Stan (Junior) Goodall and Clayton Moss.

Other sources put Willie Richardson, Donald Somerville and Norman 'Moose' Caldwell there as well, bringing the total up to 5 officers and 63 men. So a complete list would look like this:

The Officers
Major M.L. Tucker from Montreal, Quebec
Lieutenant R.J. Kennedy, Dunrobbin, Ontario
Lieutenant J.B. Cronyn, London, Ontario,
Lieutenant R.S. Tate, Toronto, Ontario
Lieutenant James Russell Martin, Meaford, Ontario

The NCO's

CSM H.S.R. Humphreys, Winnipeg, Manitoba
Sgt. D.E. Barnes, Saint John, New Brunswick
Sgt. W.G. Willick, Bothwell, Ontario
Sgt. S.R. Morris, Trinity, Newfoundland
Sgt. Gilliard, Port Stanley, Ontario
L/Sgt. J.P. Lee, Glace Bay, Nova Scotia
L/Sgt. J.W. Ogilvie, Saint John
L/Sgt. G.E. King, Truro, NS
L/Sgt. H.S. Marshall, Winnipeg
L/Sgt. S. Strong, Glace Bay, Nova Scotia
Cpl. James McLachlan, Boissevain, Manitoba
Cpl. Louis Riehl, Stratford, Ontario
Cpl. S.F. Smith, Sydney, Nova Scotia
Cpl. J.F. McCrady, Regina, Saskatchewan
Cpl. J. McDowall, Toronto, Ontario
Cpl. G.L. Robinson, Regina, Saskatchewan
Cpl. J.W. Gambling, Toronto
L/Cpl Daniel Ryan
L/Cpl. Dave Gunness, Strathroy, Ontario
L/Cpl. Dave MacDonald, Flin Flon, Manitoba
L/Cpl. J.E. Wilson, Saint John, New Brunswick
L/Cpl. A. Barbaro, Ottawa, Ontario
L/Cpl. B.E. Watling, Saint John, New Brunswick
L/Cpl. H.B. Albright, Saint John, New Brunswick
L/Cpl. H.D. Gillis, Saint John, New Brunswick
L/Cpl. J.L. Bryden, Glace Bay, Nova Scotia
L/Cpl. H.G. West, Toronto, Ontario
L/Cpl G.P. Perkins, Saint John, New Brunswick

Sappers:

G. Bigelow, Cardston, Alberta
Harold Barr, Mountain Grove, Ontario
Frost, Spanish, Ontario
Shailes, Stranraer, Saskatchewan
I. Cornell, Windsor, Ontario
McNulty, Toronto, Ontario
R.H. Rushton, Truro, Nova Scotia

E.J. Diment, Toronto, Ontario

A.M. Atchison, Toronto, Ontario

A.E. Sagar, Nippawan, BC

A.G. Thomas, Sudbury, Ontario

P.K. Mulligan, Kinkora, PEI

S. Beauchamp, Sudbury, Ontario

W.H. Davis, London, Ontario

A. Bovair, Toronto, Ontario

Le Bouthillier, St. Bernadette PQ

D.J. McCready, Pincher Creek, Alberta

G.E. Ford, Windsor, Ontario

A.B. Dale, Toronto, Ontario

Harold C. Magnusson

Leslie Joseph Roherty, Belledune River, NB

D.L.G. Hope

N.A. Thompson

Ronald Tracy Mckee

J.W. Black, Toronto, ON

D.E. Francis Toronto, ON

J.P. LeToqueux, London, ON

V.C. Titus, Centreville, ON

Stan (Junior) Goodall, Toronto, ON

Clayton Moss, Truro, N.S.

Norman (Moose) Caldwell, St. Stephen, NB

Willie Richardson, Pembrooke, ON

Donald T. Somerville, Ridgetown, ON

Medical

L/Cpl. Roseborouh, North Bay, Ontario

Spr. E.S. MacDonald, Swayerville, Ontario

Attached from ICAT, Captain. Mongeon R.C. Padre

Appendix #2:

The Maintenance Party: The Men of the 10th Field Park, RCE Who Took Part in Op. Berlin

No. 1 Section: (attached to the 20th Field Company, RCE)

N.C.O. i/c - B29575 L/Sgt. W.K. Teed

Engine Fitters - B32118 L/Cpl. J.R. Marrett

M26926 Spr. K.M. Rea

L 8315 Spr. G.R. MacDonald

A102715 Spr. P. McShane

Electrician - F79081 Spr. R.W. Hebb

No. 2 Section: (attached to the 23rd Field Company, RCE)

N.C.O. i/c - B110973 L/Sgt. B.O. Plowright

Engine Fitters - L51483 l/CPl. A.R. Gamble

M26920 Spr. L.E. Hocpfer

B25789 Spr. W.J. Woolley

B26781 Spr. E.R. Fisher

Electrician - F89606 Spr. A.J. Ellis

Appendix #3:

Timings

Timings for the Eastern Evacuation Site
2050 hrs - 23rd Field Company, RCE arrives in the orchard

2100 hrs - barrage begins

2130 hrs - assault boats from the 260th Field Company, R.E. are in the water

- Storm boat #1 is in the water and immediately sinks

2140 hrs - the first assault boat reaches the north bank

2145 hrs - Storm boat #2 is launched

2215 hrs - Storm boat #3 is launched

2235 hrs - Storm boat #4 is launched and the others are launched roughly 20 minutes apart

0330 hrs - Storm boat #14 is launched with Cpl. Robinson in command

0545 hrs - Lt. Col. Henniker calls off the operation - the 23rd had made approximately 150 trips

0740 hrs- Lt. Kennedy finally reaches the south bank

1030 hrs - Lt. Cronyn ends his search for missing personnel and returns to base

Timings for the Western Evacuation Site
2100 hrs - barrage begins

2130 hrs - assault boats from the 553rd Field Company, R.E. are in the water

2140 hrs - the first assault boat reaches the far side

2330 hrs - one assault boat was sent over to see if they was any one on the north bank

0100 hrs - operations suspended for an hour due to friendly fire

0200 hrs - another assault boat was sent over

0300 hrs - the evacuation is called off in this area

0330 hrs - orders to send four Storm boats to the eastern area 1500 yards away

Appendix #4

The Casualties

Killed in action:

Lt. J.R. Martin

F22448 L/Cpl. Ryan, W.D.

G53227 Spr. Hope, D.L.G.

G53226 Spr. Magnusson, H.C.

F91044 Spr. Thompson, N.A.

Missing and presumed killed in action:

G6257 Spr. Roherty, L.J.

Died of wounds received:

G13145 Spr. McKee, R.T.

Wounded:

P10915 Sgt. Barnes, D.E.

B40386 Spr. Francis, D.E.

B40393 Spr. LeToqueux, J.P.

B400393 Spr. McCready, D.J.

It is estimated that ninety-five men of the British 1st Airborne Division lost their lives during the evacuation. A large number of them drowned.

Appendix #5

Nominal Roll 20th Field Company, Royal Canadian Engineers
30 September 1944

Major A.W. Jones
Capt. W.H. Parsons
Lt. W.W. Gemmell
Lt. B.J.F. Hamilton
Lt. D.C. Holland
Lt. O.T. Linton
Lt. G.A. Mackie

H36676 CSM Cameron CT
H93313 CQMS Owen BJ

B28862 Sgt Aseltine RW
B28731 Sgt Dorzinsky CJ
M59040 Sgt Hovan AS
H82080 Sgt Jensen H
L41084 Sgt Ollis ES

H93490 L/Sgt King RJ
H93451 L/Sgt Nielson KA
H93329 L/Sgt Simm JW
H93506 L/Sgt Thomsen PC
H93328 L/Sgt Rodgers W
H93314 L/Sgt Ward VG
H93522 L/Sgt Whitaker JJ

H13081 Cpl Bramwell GE
H93440 A/Cpl Hamilton IJ
H93489 Cpl Moller HE
H93456 Cpl Moore GW
C16548 Cpl Mullis SH
B43150 Cpl Murray HM
H93507 Cpl McIvor CJ
H93511 Cpl Mclean SA
H93510 Cpl Peden NR
H93516 Cpl Pitre JC

H93330 Cpl Reid WA
H93475 A/Cpl Robbins RH
H36418 Cpl Scott PE
H93315 Cpl Spencer RF
H93312 Cpl Ward CH

F95010 L/Cpl Basquil JS
B29712 A/L/Cpl Best AJ
H93505 L/Cpl Brouillette EJA
H93418 L/Cpl Cantlon RT
C100317 L/Cpl Coleman CL
H93480 L/Cpl Dalman NA
L91653 L/Cpl Duncan WE
H93311 L/Cpl Elko JS
H93529 L/Cpl Ferguson WH
L91704 L/Cpl Foster CN
F23427 L/Cpl Hamilton H
H93520 L/Cpl Martel WA
F23355 A/ L/Cpl McInrtye AP
L91708 L/Cpl Nurse CGNF
F23358 L/Cpl O'Brien DS
H93503 L/Cpl Petersen KA
H93441 L/Cpl Sanders LP
L92960 A/ L/Cpl Smith AC
B113567 L/Cpl Thomson WA
M59409 A/ L/Cpl White J

L104665 Sapper Abood G
H93437 Sapper Adams J
F40222 Pte Andrews LM
H93532 Sapper Armstrong GA
L92918 Sapper Auld JM

H82045 Sapper Barker LH
L91616 Sapper Beaton JG

F79819 Pte Beaver V GC
H93322 Sapper Beckett KR
C2784 Sapper Belaire MI
L92968 Sapper Bellamy AP
L91701 Sapper Bellamy NA
L92958 Sapper Beng Meo
H93460 Sapper Bennett S
B22649 Sapper Bird NF
L92972 Sapper Blondeau EG
H82191 Sapper Boyce EW
H93416 Sapper Bredeson HI
B22673 Sapper Broeko MJ
H82170 Sapper Brouillette PJ
M7116 Sapper Brown EP
H93382 Sapper Bueckert JI
D129803 Sapper Burke TJ
M28183 Sapper Burns GV

M105600 Pte Cake HC
F51029 Sapper Caldwell BD
L92909 Sapper Campbell AE
H100752 Sapper Campbell GT
K71245 Sapper Cantlon DV
H93444 Pte Carr JA
L91707 Sapper Chepeur J
F31114 Sapper Chisholm JL
F75996 Sapper Clark LG
K40974 Sapper Cole SE
H93404 Sapper Comrie HW
H93481 Sapper Copping AR
F51032 Sapper Corkum AL
F59620 Sapper Costello LJ
L92965 Sapper Craig CM
H93321 Sapper Cunnungham J

L27560 Sapper Davis GA
L41460 Pte Davis J
H93361 Sapper Dearden JR
L92973 Sapper Densley AH
L91640 Sapper Desjardins LJ
H93533 Sapper Dickson Rj
L91702 Sapper Donaldson W
H82081 Sapper Doncaster JM

H93308 Sapper Dowhy W
K16254 Sapper Doyle MP
M59424 Sapper Edkins JE
L91658 Sapper Egoroff GV

M38356 Sapper Elaschuk N
F65219 Sapper Ernst CF
H93430 Sapper Falzarano J
L66371 Sapper Feist LV
L102374 Sapper Fenty K
H93376 Sapper Ferley M
H8471 Sapper Fidler S
F5433 Sapper Fylnn JT

B130233 Sapper Gair H
B138102 Sapper Genois AL
H93542 Sapper Gilbert GAA
H100356 Sapper Grieve DL
H93391 Sapper Gudmundson B
F41013 Sapper Guiderson RH
H93384 Sapper Gustafson ANG
H93373 Sapper Gwiazda M

F22470 Sapper Hall TMS
L102409 Sapper Hanson HE
H204555 Sapper Harasymew W
H93324 Sapper Hargreaves E
H93346 Hay WN
H93425 Sapper Haydon JL
H93494 Sapper Heinzig P
H82287 Sapper Henry JS
H93526 Sapper Heppner H
L91670 Sapper Herron JD
H93381 Sapper Hogg J
H93493 Sapper Holgate WT
H93380 Sapper Holt KR
H93309 Sapper Howell OW
L91719 Sapper Hudymka S
L91667 Sapper Hunt TW

D56718 Sapper Imbeault EJA
E28237 Sapper Ireland B

K75176 Sapper Jensen EJ
L2791 Sapper Johnson CW
L91641 Sapper Johnson WA
L100795 Sapper Johnston HE
H93340 Sapper Jordi O
G49993 Sapper Judge RD

H93352 Sapper Kafara W
L101814 Sapper Keller MG
A20469 Sapper Kellestine GW
H93473 Sapper Kennedy WE
K70039 Sapper Keogh CP
F40242 Pte King RE
L91672 Sapper Knott DW
H67528 Sapper Kuhn R
M36422 Sapper Kupchiak FF

B131170 Sapper Leach TJ
F77878 Sapper Leadbetter RP
H93442 Sapper Lietz VC
F23406 Sapper Little JD
M102531 Sapper Lockert C
L12516 Sapper Lugrin WL
L91663 Sapper Lutz PEP

K71643 Sapper Machin RG
L91668 Sapper Major GJ
K45504 Sapper Maksymchuk T
L92974 Sapper Matthews WR
H82048 Sapper Melnychuk N
F3926 Sapper Menzies DH
H63883 Sapper Metcalf AL
C125040 Sapper Moore WS
M36533 Sapper Morrow NM
H93448 Sapper Mullin RW
H93420 Sapper Murray AC
L91671 Sapper McCredie JNE
F22435 Sapper McDaniel PH
F23320 Sapper MacDonald WB
M103739 Sapper Mckay J
F22382 Sapper Mackeigan AJ
F22421 Sapper Mackenzie CR
F32241 Sapper Mcleod AE

M107624 Sapper Mcmullin DW
H195186 Sapper Mcpherson RH
H93513 Sapper Mcrae GN
M107609 Sapper Mctighe GJ

B130321 Sapper Nicoll J
F86314 Sapper Nicoll WW
L91617 Sapper Nordstrom CN

H93531 Sapper O'Callaghan WM

D129990 Sapper Pepin JEM
L19774 Sapper Peters WW
H93343 Sapper Petrie J
D129775 Sapper Piche JP
B113222 Sapper Pinnell EGE
F64832 Sapper Pitman AE
H103743 Sapper Pitre EG
L91666 Sapper Pollard AMNR
H93323 Sapper Proud DJ

L91665 Sapper Rau TC
H93399 Sapper Reichert MJ
B144337 Sapper Reid WW
B22674 Sapper Ressel FS
L92963 Sapper Rimmer WM
F32860 Sapper Roberts MJ
L63281 Sapper Rondquist WH
H93535 Sapper Rose KP
H93443 Sapper Ross BW
H93497 Sapper Ralo RW

F9152 Sapper Sanderson RG
D15055 Sapper Sauve M
L92916 Sapper Schappert RG
F91779 Sapper Schofield EO
B25257 Sapper Scriver C
F66269 Pte Selvage JF
L104401 Sapper Sielsky MM
L91633 Sapper Sigouin J
H93359 Sapper Sigurdson AS
B130985 Sapper Sindrey WP
L91642 Sapper Stone RA

H36629 Sapper Strachan DN
K73253 Sapper Surina AP
E19368 Sapper Surcliffe JP

H82046 Sapper Tetroe HJ
G15015 Sapper Thibodeau MJ
B97214 Sapper Thicke HD
G4576 Sapper Tims WB
H93354 Sapper Topolewski N
L92957 Sapper Trobak OJ

L91645 Sapper Vermeulen AE
C100324 Sapper Vollrath EW

H93433 Sapper Waterman GW
F51024 Sapper Webber DM
H103637 Sapper Weber AA
M104080 Sapper Wegreen WE
L101453 Sapper Weishaupt J
L91710 Sapper Westling AO
H101651 Sapper Wiley PE
L97004 Sapper Wilkinson JJ
A103379 Sapper Wilson NJ
A103324 Sapper Wilson RM
F76579 Sapper Worth MG

Appendix #6

Storm Boat Crews and Their Functions

A report entitled, `Review of Org. of storm boats assault drill. Based on experiences of the 23rd Field Company, R.C.E. at Arnhem' it defines the 3 crew members as the following:

Coxswain: is in command of the boat including all passengers while they are aboard, and will operate the outboard motor.

Boatman: supervise the loading and trim of the boat, will guide the boat while it is under way and will assist the shoreman in shoving off and fending off. He must be capable of spelling off the coxswain.

Shoreman: is responsible for reporting to the sec comd when the boat is launched and each time it completes a trip, for reporting to the sec comd when fuel is low or cas. occur, for guiding passengers allotted to the boat from the infantry control to the crossing point, for pushing off on departure and for fending off an arrival.

Appendix #7

The Equipment:

Assault Boat Mk. III

A collapsible canvas boat which is used to carry an infantry section and their weapons across in an assault river crossing. It is propelled by paddling or by hauling on a ferry line from the bank. It has a stiff plywood bottom, canvas sides and a stiff timber gunwale. When in use, several struts secure the gunwales to the bottom of the boat. It has the benefit of rope carrying handles along the sides of the boat.

The Storm Boat

A shallow draft assault boat 20'0" in length and 6'-6" wide with an oak frame and plywood bottom. It weighed 800 pounds empty and was powered by a 50-HP outboard motor which weighed 198 pounds. Its speed was 6 knots loaded and 20 knots unladen and designed to operate on wide fast rivers that are opposed by the enemy.

Evinrude model #8008

A High Speed, 4 Cylinder, 2 cycle motor that was designed for use with the Army Storm Boat. 50 HP with no reverse. Fuel mixture: mix 1 pint of SAE No. 50 body oil with each gallon of gasoline in clean fuel container and thoroughly mix before pouring into motor's 28 Pts. fuel tank. It was 72"x31"x32" and weighted 198 pounds.

Appendix #8

Lessons Learned

Stated in the 43rd Division's War Diary are these points:

1) In spite of all one's endeavors a great many assault boats got lost and it is not sound to rely on the same boats on successive nights.

    Men must be properly warned of our fire plan so that they do not confuse its noise with that of enemy fire.

2) Men not actually employed must be concentrated in one place before they dig in. Otherwise they get to ground all over the place and when wanted cannot be found.

3) Stouthearted RE commanders must be restrained from continually crossing and recrossing the river themselves. At the start their example is priceless, but when once started, the Commander's task is to supervise all the arrangements from the assembly point down to the river and this cannot be done from a boat in midstream.

Lieutenant-Colonel Henniker signed the report on October 4th 1944. It obviously applies mostly to the Royal Engineers and not to the 23rd or the 20th Field Companies, R.C.E. Except for point #2, the 23rd were well ahead of the other companies. Granted, #1 did not apply to them, but their experience in this type of work kept Major Tucker and all of his men where they needed to be.

The commanding officer of the 20th Field Company, RCE, Major A.W. Jones, reported these points a few days after the operation:

1) Storm boats were NOT practical when in close contact with the enemy and no covering fire was allowed.

2) Two assault crossings had been made on the two nights preceding this operation, hence the enemy had the spot well marked and covered by machine gun posts.

3) Assault boats were the answer because they could be launched and manned without excessive noise.

4) If motor propelled craft have to be used in such an operation, it is suggested that better engines and prop units replace Evinrudes as much difficulty was experienced with the Evinrudes stalling when their props fouled in the mud.

5) Some kind of signal should be offered from the far bank such as a

flash light to indicated the exact position of the troops. We had 300 yards of beach to comb and on that beach were three enemy machine gun posts situated up above the flood banks.

6) In all such operations, there should be an absolute minimum of personnel on hand. We started off with 12 sections but this was soon cut down to 4. All the remaining sections were sent back to a point of safety to rest and await further orders. This is one of the reasons why no casualties were experienced, all personnel being under complete control.

In early October, the 23rd came up with a way of water-proofing the Evinrude motors and had worked out a method of transporting storm boats with carrying bars. They would slide metal bars through rope loops attached to the boats. The other company in the ICAT, the 5th Field Company, R.C.E. carried out a series of tests on how to be move a storm boat. Several teams of men each used a different method.

On October 26th, the other company in the ICAT, RCE, the 5th Field Company, R.C.E. carried out a series of tests on how to move a Storm boat. Several teams of men each used a different method. The results clearly show that using the new method designed by the 23rd was the quickest and least exhausting of all the methods. This was the basis for the report submitted to Colonel Bermingham on 26 October 1944.

The maintenance party had this to say:

In a normal ops, especially during daylight, it is suggested that this party take the form of one adv. Wksp. Det. [advance workshop detail] per coy. It is suggested that it should be carried in one 3 ton truck, and made up as follows:

NCO i/c of detail
Driver
4 Engine Fitters,
1 Electrician
2 Carpenters
1 Welder with gas Welding equipment
Plus 1 Lance Corporal in charge of 2 men for petrel party
2 extra men for carrying party.

They would be self contained for duration of operation and have in their lorry all equipment and stores necessary for engine and boat repairs.

Appendix #9

Code Names for The Special Bridging Force During Operation Market Garden

If the bridges are blown and there is no opposition, then use:
  'Harry' for the Maas River and Serials R735 to 741 for 878 vehicles.
  'Jim' for the W. Canal and Serials R742 to 746 for 843 vehicles.
  'Michael' for the Waal River and Serials R747 to 754 for 380 vehicles.
  'Peter' for the Neder Rijn and Serials R755 to 760 for 536 vehicles.

If all goes well and the column is required for the Ijessel River then use:
  'Richard' with Serials R761 to 768 for 766 vehicles.

If a single bridge is blown and there is no opposition, then use:
  'Maurice' for the Maas River and Serials R769 to 775 for 1110 vehicles.
  'George' for the W. Canal and Serials R776 to 778 for 566 vehicles.
  'Spike' for the Waal River and Serials R779 to 784 for 1486 vehicles.
  'John' for the Neder Rijn and Serials R785 to 790 for 1146 vehicles.

If bridges are held by the enemy and the columns are needed by the 43rd Division, for a single brigade crossing then use:
  'Tom' for the Maas River and Serials R720 to 722 for 300 vehicles.
  'Fred' for the Neder Rijn and Serials R720 to 722 for 300 vehicles.
  'Bessie' for the Waal River and Serials R727 to 728 for 309 vehicles.

If bridges are held by the enemy and the columns are needed by the 43rd Division for a two brigade crossing then use:
  'Bill' for the Maas River and Serials R723 to 726 for 419 vehicles.
  'Bertram' for the Neder Rijn and Serials R723 to 726 for 419 vehicles.
  'Basil' for the Waal River and Serials R729 to 732 for 316 vehicles.

Appendix #10
Bertram Column
(taken from the 85 Bridge Coy, RCASC War Diary)

Bertram Column was composed as the following:

R-724 - `L' (raft) platoon

R-725 - *Company HQ less small rear party*
- *1 section of workshop*
- *`K' (FBE) platoon*
- *14 loads (42 boats in total) of Storm Boats carried by the 551st G.T. Company*

R-726 - *7 loads (42 engines) of Evinrude engines carried by the 551st G.T. Company*
- *8 units of Sommerfeld track carried by the 551st G.T. Company*
- *4 units of Assault boats carried by the 128th Bridge Company*
- *1624 (Bailey Bridging) platoon of the 106th Bridge Company*
- *1625 (Bailey Bridging) platoon of the 128th Bridge Company*
- *1641 (Bailey Bridging) platoon of the 147th Bridge Company*
- *1636 (FBE) platoon of the 128th Bridge Company*
- *2 units of Grillage carried by the 551st G.T. Company*
- *3 units of ramp carried by the 551st G.T. Company*

Appendix #11

Bertram Column Details
(taken from the 10th Fd. Pk. RCE War Diary)

The bridging units were assigned the following:

Detail No. 1 *(To support the 204th Field Company, RE)*
   Consisting 4 assault boat units from 551 G.T. Coy. and a M/
   Tug from 1625 Platoon, 106st Bridge Coy.

Detail No. 2 *(to support 260th Field Company, RE)*
   Consisting 16 vehicles from `L' Platoon, 85 Bridge Coy,
   RCASC to carry 4 close support rafts.

Detail No. 3 *(to support 20th Field Company, RCE)*
   1624 (Bailey Pontoon) platoon less landing bay, 106 Bridge Coy.
   1 landing bay from 1625 Platoon, 106 Bridge Coy.
   2 sections of bailey bridging from 1641 Platoon, 147 Bridge Coy.

Detail No. 4 *(to support 23rd Field Company, RCE)*
   6 loads (36 engines) of Evinrude engines carried by 551st G.T. Coy.
   12 loads (36 boats) of storm boats carried by 551st G.T. Coy.

Detail No. 5
   5 Bulldozers (2 from 10th Fd. Park, 1 from 43rd Div.)
   13 tippers of pioneers
   8 Sommerfeld track units carried by 551st G.T. Coy.

Detail No. 6
   `J' (FBE) Platoon, 85 Bridge Coy
   1636 (FBE) Platoon, 128 Bridge Coy.

Detail No. 7 (Recce Party)
   Capt. Labelle and Lt. Agro (from 85th Bridge Coy.) will report
   to Major Evill of the 204th Fd. Coy. to scout for a location for
   lorries to met once off-loaded.

End Notes:

1 -   p179 `Arnhem' by Urquhart
2 -   Article: `23rd Field Company Engineers accomplish dangerous tasks on Europe's trail of duress' by Capt. Jack Golding in the Ma ple Leaf Paper
3 -   Official War Diary, 260th Field Company, Royal Engineers
4 -   Interviewed by Author
5 -   Interviewed by Author
6 -   `The Twenty-Third Story' by Mike Tucker and the 23rd Field Com pany, RCE
7 -   `The Twenty-Third Story' by Mike Tucker and the 23rd Field Com pany, RCE
8 -   `Whispers and Shadows' by Russ Kennedy
9 -   `The Grey Goose of Arnhem' by Leo Heaps
10 - `Whispers and Shadows' by Russ Kennedy
11 - Interviewed by Author
12 - `The Twenty-Third Story' by Mike Tucker and the 23rd Field Com pany, RCE
13 - `Whispers and Shadows' by Russ Kennedy
14 - `The Twenty-Third Story' by Mike Tucker and the 23rd Field Com pany, RCE
15 - `Whispers and Shadows' by Russ Kennedy
16 - War Diary, 23rd Field Company, Royal Canadian Engineers
17 - `The Twenty-Third Story' by Mike Tucker and the 23rd Field Com pany, RCE
18 - `The Twenty-Third Story' by Mike Tucker and the 23rd Field Com pany, RCE
19 - `The Twenty-Third Story' by Mike Tucker and the 23rd Field Com pany, RCE
20 - War Diary, 23rd Field Company, Royal Canadian Engineers
21 - War Diary, 23rd Field Company, Royal Canadian Engineers
22 - Interviewed by Author
23 - War Diary, 23rd Field Company, Royal Canadian Engineers
24 - War Diary, 85 Cdn Bridge Coy. - RCASC
25 - Interviewed by Author
26 - War Diary, 23rd Field Company, Royal Canadian Engineers
27 - `Whispers and Shadows' by Russ Kennedy
28 - `Whispers and Shadows' by Russ Kennedy
29 - War Diary, 85 Cdn Bridge Coy. - RCASC
30 - `Whispers and Shadows' by Russ Kennedy
31 - `Whispers and Shadows' by Russ Kennedy

32 - 'The Twenty-Third Story' by Mike Tucker and the 23rd Field Company, RCE

33 - Newspaer Article: 'Sarnians played pivotal role in real Bridge Too Far Battle' by Paul Egan '1992' of the observer

34 - Regimental History 85 Cdn. Bridge Coy. June 1941 - May 1941

35 - Interviewed by Author

36 - Interviewed by Author

37 - Interviewed by Author

38 - 'Incident at Arnhem' by Charles Lynden

39 - 'Official War Diary, 43rd Wessex Division'

40 - 'An Image Of War' by Lt-Colonel Mark Henniker

41 - 'An Image Of War' by Lt-Colonel Mark Henniker

42 - 'The Twenty-Third Story' by Mike Tucker and the 23rd Field Company, RCE

43 - 'Canadian Role At Arnhem Seldom Acknowledged in Stories' by Lt. John B. Cronyn

44 - 2 CER records at Camp Petawawa

45 - War Diary, 23rd Field Company, Royal Canadian Engineers

46 - 'Whispers and Shadows' by Russ Kennedy

47 - 'Whispers and Shadows' by Russ Kennedy

48 - 'Canadian Role At Arnhem Seldom Acknowledged in Stories' by Lt. John B. Cronyn

49 - 'The Glider Gang' by Milton Dank

50 - 'Canadian Role At Arnhem Seldom Acknowledged in Stories' by Lt. John B. Cronyn

51 - War Diary, 23rd Field Company, Royal Canadian Engineers

52 - Interviewed by Author

53 - Interviewed by Author

54 - Newspaer Article: 'Sarnians played pivotal role in real Bridge Too Far Battle' by Paul Egan '1992' of the observer

55 - 'Canadian Role At Arnhem Seldom Acknowledged in Stories' by Lt. John B. Cronyn

56 - 'Canadians at War'

57 - 2 CER records at Camp Petawawa

58 - Interviewed by Author

59 - 'Canadian Role At Arnhem Seldom Acknowledged in Stories' by Lt. John B. Cronyn

60 - War Diary, 43rd Wessex Division

61 - 'The Race For The Rhine Bridges' by Alexander McKee

62 - 2 CER records at Camp Petawawa

63 - Official War Diary, 20th Field Company, Royal Canadian Engineers

64 - 'The Race For The Rhine Bridges' by Alexander McKee

65 - Interviewed by Author

66 - 'The Island' by Tim Saunders

67 - 'An Image Of War' by Lt-Colonel Mark Henniker

68 - Official War Diary, 260th Field Company, Royal Engineers

69 - `The Glider Gang' by Milton Dank
70 - `An Image Of War' by Lt-Colonel Mark Henniker
71 - `Whispers and Shadows' by Russ Kennedy
72 - War Diary, 23rd Field Company, Royal Canadian Engineers
73 - `An Image Of War' by Lt-Colonel Mark Henniker
74 - Interviewed by Author
75 - `Die nacht ben ik een ander mens geworden' from the Betuwe newspaper, The Netherlands – an interview with Sgt. Sandy Morris and Moose Caldwell.
76 - `Die nacht ben ik een ander mens geworden' from the Betuwe newspaper, The Netherlands – an interview with Sgt. Sandy Morris and Moose Caldwell.
77 - `Canadian Role At Arnhem Seldom Acknowledged in Stories' by Lt. John B. Cronyn
78 - `Arnhem' by Christopher Hibbert
79 - `Arnhem' by General Urquhart
80 - `Arnhem' by General Urquhart
81 - `An Image Of War' by Lt-Colonel Mark Henniker
82 - K. Margry p 684.
83 - `Arnhem Battle Research Group' records
84 - `Arnhem Battle Research Group' records
85 - Interviewed by Author
86 - `Canadian Role At Arnhem Seldom Acknowledged in Stories' by Lt. John B. Cronyn
87 - interviewed by Author
88 - Interviewed by Author
89 - Grodzinski Letters)
90 - War Diary of 3 Cdn. E + M Sec (A)
91 - `A Bridge Too Far' by C. Ryan
92 - `A Bridge Too Far' by C. Ryan
93 - `Arnhem' by Martin Midllebrook
94 - p586 `A Bridge Too Far' by C. Ryan
95 - p587 `A Bridge Too Far' by C. Ryan
96 - `Off At Last' Robert Sigmond
97 - War Diary, 4th Para. Sq., RE
98 - Letter of Recommendations by CO's from Public Record Office, London UK
98a– Captain Brown's account
99 - `Whispers and Shadows' by Russ Kennedy
100 - `Remember Arnhem' by John Fiarley
101 - Official War Diary, 260th Field Company, Royal Engineers
102 - `An Image Of War' by Lt-Colonel Mark Henniker
103 - Interviewed by Author
104 - `Whispers and Shadows' by Russ Kennedy
105 - `Arnhem Battle Research Group' records
106 - `Whispers and Shadows' by Russ Kennedy
107 - Interviewed by Author

108 - `An Image Of War' by Lt-Colonel Mark Henniker

109 - `An Image Of War' by Lt-Colonel Mark Henniker

110 - `Canadian Role At Arnhem Seldom Acknowledged in Stories' by Lt. John B. Cronyn

111 - `Arnhem Battle Research Group' records

112 - `Arnhem Battle Research Group' records

113 - `With Spanders Descending' by Joe Roberts

114 - `Whispers and Shadows' by Russ Kennedy

115 - `The Island' by Tim Saunders

116 - Film, `Theirs Is The Glory' 1945

117 - `Arnhem 1944: The Airborne Battle' by Martin Middlebrook

118 - `Canadian Role At Arnhem Seldom Acknowledged in Stories' by Lt. John B. Cronyn

119 - `Canadian Role At Arnhem Seldom Acknowledged in Stories' by Lt. John B. Cronyn

120 - Interviewed by Author

121 - Lt. Kennedy's Citation

122 - `The Twenty-Third Story' by Mike Tucker and the 23rd Field Company, RCE

124 - Interviewed by Author

125 - Interviewed by Author

126 - `Die nacht ben ik een ander mens geworden' from the Betuwe newspaper, The Netherlands – an interview with Sgt. Sandy Morris and Moose Caldwell.

Bibliography

2 CER records, Camp Petawawa

Arnhem Battle Research Group

Baynes, John. *Urquhart of Arnhem*. London: Brassey's, 1993

Blitz Assault-Through Fire and Water. (no author credited) London: Military Press International, 1995

Bouchery, Jean. *The Canadian Soldier*. (Alan McKay, Trans.) Paris: Histoire and Collections, 2003

Byers, A.R. *The Canadians at War 1939/45*. Montreal: Reader's Digest Association (Canada) Ltd. 1986, pg 579

Cholewczynski, George F. *Poles Apart*. New York: Sarpedon Publishers Inc. 1993

Copp, Terry. *Our Rescue Role at Arnhem*. Legion Magazine September/October 2000. http://www.legionmagazine.com/features/canadianmilitaryhistory/00-09.asp.

Cronyn, John B. *Canadian Role at Arnhem Seldom Acknowledged in Stories*. N.p. N.d.

Dank, Milton. *The Gilder Gang: An Eyewitness History of World War Two Glider Combat*. Bennington, VT.: Merriam Press, 1999

Die nacht ben ik een ander mens geworden. The Netherlands. Betuwe, n.d. An interview with Sgt. Sandy Morris and Moose Caldwell

Egan, Paul. *Sarnians played pivotal role in real Bridge Too Far Battle*. The Observer, n.d. UK, 1992

Essame, H. *The 43rd Wessex Division at War, 1944-1945*. London: William Clowes, 1952

Fairley, John. *Remember Arnhem*. Aldershot: Pegasus Journal, 1978

Golding, Jack. *23rd Field Company Engineers accomplish dangerous tasks on Europe's trial of duress*. The Maple Leaf, n.d. Ottawa: Department of National Defence

Grodzinski, John. Unpublished letters and personal correspondence with members of the Canadian rescue force.

Harclerode, Peter. *Arnhem: A Tragedy of Errors*. London: Arms and Armour Press, 1994

Heaps, Leo. *The Grey Goose of Arnhem*. London: Weidenfeld and Nicolson, 1976

Henniker, Mark. *An Image of War*. London: Leo Cooper, 1987

Hibbert, Christopher. *The Battle of Arnhem*. New York: Macmillan, 1962

Hogden, Murray. *Rescue at Arnhem*, Kingston Whig Standard, 26 September 1999

Holmes, Ken J. *History of the Corps of Royal Canadian Engineers Volume II* Nepean, Ont.: Military Engineering Institute of Canada, 1997

Kennedy, Russ and Elizabeth (Kennedy) Marsh *Boats, Bridges & Valour: The 23rd Field Company, Royal Canadian Engineers in WWII*. 2008

Kennedy, Russ. *Whispers and Shadows: Arnhem Fifty Years Later*. Kingston, Ont.: privately pub.

Kerry, A.J. and W.A. McDill. *History of the Corps of Royal Canadian Engineers Volume II* Nepean, Ont.: Military Engineering Institute of Canada, 1966.

Kershaw, Robert J. *It Never Snows in September*. Shepperton: Ian Allan Ltd. 1994

Korthals, A., Margry, K. Thuring, G., and Voskuil, R. September 1944. (M.E. Zuidgeest-Perquin, M.)

Grotenhuis-Huisken and P.H. Luijten, Trans.) Weesp: Fibula-Van Dishoeck. 1984

Lynden, Charles. *Incident at Arnhem*. N.p, n.d.

Margry, Karl ed. *Operation Market Garden Then And Now Volume 1 & 2*. Battle of Britain International Ltd. 2002

Middlebrook, Martin. *Arnhem 1944: The Airborne Battle*, 17-26 September. London: Penguin Books Ltd, 1994

Mckee, Alexander. *The Race for the Rhine Bridge*. New York: Stein & Day, 1945

Medical War Diary, 43rd Wessex Division

Powell, Geoffrey. *The Devil's Birthday*. London: Leo Cooper, 1992

Powell, Geoffrey. *Men at Arnhem*. London: Leo Cooper, 2003

Pronk, Patrick. Airborne Engineers, The Shiny 9th: An Illustrated History of the 9th (Airborne) Field Company Royal Engineers 1939-1945. Renkum, UK: R.N. Sigmond, 2001

Provisional Working Instructions for Storm Boat 20ft, MK I. Ottawa Ministry of Supply & Services, Aug. 1944

Public Record Office, London. Letters of Recommendation from Commanders

Rafting and Bridging Military Training Pamphlet No. 74 Part III: Assault Crossing Equipment (1944) Ottawa: DND, Jan. 1944

Regimental History, 85 Canadian Bridge Company, June 1944—May 1945. N.p, n.d.

Roberts, Joseph. With Spanders Descending: A History of the Royal Electrical and Mechanical Engineers with 1st Airborne Division, 1942-1945. Liverpool: Bluecoat Press, 1996

Ryan, Cornelius. *A Bridge Too Far*. New York: Simon and Schuster, 1974

Saunders, Tim. *The Island: Nijmegen to Arnhem. (Battleground Europe)*, S. Yorkshire: Pen & Sword Books

Sigmond, Robert. Off At Last: An Illustrated History of the 7th (Galway) Battalion, the King's Own Scottish Borderers, 1939-1945. Privately pub., 1997

Tucker, Mike. The Twenty-Third Story. Privately published, n.p., n.d.

Urquhart, R.E. Arnhem. London: White Lion Pub., 1973

War Diary, H.Q. 1 Canadian Army Troops Engineers

War Diary, 10th Field Park Company, Royal Canadian Engineers

War Diary, 20th Field Company, Royal Canadian Engineers

War Diary, 23rd Field Company, Royal Canadian Engineers

War Diary, 43rd Wessex Division Engineers

War Diary, 204th Field Company, Royal Engineers

War Diary, 207th Field Park Company, Royal Engineers

War Diary, 260th Field Company, Royal Engineers

War Diary, 551st General Transport Company, R.A.S.C.

War Diary, 553rd Field Company, Royal Engineers

Index

The author listening to Russ Kennedy at his cottage
in the summer of 2009. (Laura Sliz)

About the Author

John Sliz was born and raised in Toronto, Canada. He became fascinated with Operation Market Garden after he read, `A Bridge Too Far' at the age of nine. Many years later, a visit to Arnhem in the summer of 2001 only added fuel to the fire, eventually resulting in the publication of `The Storm Boat Kings'. While researching this book and waiting for its publication, he wrote a small book on the engineer equipment that was used during the operation. `Engineer Assault Boats In Canadian Service' was published in December 2006 by Service Publications. Vanwell Publishing finally published the first edition of `Storm Boat Kings' in 2009. The above photo of the author listening to Russ Kennedy was taken shortly after the book's release.

Since then he has written a lot more books, including four novels, three travel books and ten books of the Market Garden Engineer Series. He currently lives in Oshawa, Ontario and is busy researching engineers in World War II when he is not playing drums, guitar or designing electrical systems.

For more information or to contact him please email him at: thesliz@hotmail.com

More books
on the

23rd Field
Company, Royal Canadian
Engineers by John Sliz

Boats at Arnhem and Other Stories

Boats at Arnhem, The Storm Boat Kings, Bob Tate's Bridge Into the
Apple Orchard, The Night Waal Crossing, The 10th A.G.R.E. During
Operation Market Garden, A Popular Guide to the German Army
(Engineers), Bridging the Gap: Olafson Infantry Footbridge, The
Martin Bridge, Royal Canadian Engineers' Tests and 1st Canadian
Corps Signals.

ISBN: 978-1-927679-08-1

The Long Road Back to Arnhem

*The 23rd Field Company, R.C.E. in The Netherlands and Germany
1944 and 1945*

Pegasus II: The Storm Boat Kings' Perspective, Like Clockwork: The
US 101st Airborne Leaves the Island, A Bridge on a Bridge: the Spider
Web Bridge on the Nijmegen Railway Bridge, Operation Noah: The
Emergency Evacuation of the Island November 1944, His Majesty Ca-
nadian Pile Driver 'Spike' Bermingham, Storm Boat School, Special
Boat Section: M.I.9 and the Storm Boat Kings, Road Work, Nijmegen
Power Station and the Death of a Sapper, Back to Arnhem: the Twenty-
third's Part in operation Anger, Bridges at Arnhem and Other Places,
Storm Boat Victory: The 23rd Field Company, R.C.E. at the Nijmegen
Regatta June 1945 and Disbandment.

ISBN: 978-1-927679-82-8

The
Market Garden Engineer
Series by John Sliz

The Wrong Side of the River
The Polish Engineer Company at Arnhem
ISBN: 978-09783838-0-0

Basic Function
The 4th Parachute Squadron, Royal Engineers at Arnhem
ISBN: 978-0-9783838-1-7

Engineers at the Bridge
The 1st Parachute Squadron Royal Engineers at Arnhem
ISBN: 978-0-9783838-4-8

Assault Boats on the Waal
The 307th Engineer Battalion During Operation Market Garden
ISBN: 978-09877404-

Bridging Hell's Highway
The 326th Engineer Battalion During Operation Market Garden
ISBN: 978-09877404-

A Long Tradition
The 9th (Airborne) Field Company Royal Engineers at Arnhem
ISBN: 978-09877404-4-1

A Token Force
The 261st Field Park Company Royal Engineers (Airborne) at Arnhem
ISBN: 978-0-9877404-6-5

Commander Royal Engineers
The Headquarters of the Royal Engineers at Arnhem
ISBN: 978-1-92679-04-3

Bridging the Club Route
Guards Armoured Division's Engineers During Operation Market Garden
ISBN: 978-1-927679-14-2

Special Bridging Force
Engineers Under XXX Corps During Operation Market Garden
ISBN: 978-1-927679-

All Books by John Sliz

1) *Engineer Assault Boats in Canadian Service* (2006)
2) *War History 18th Field Company, Royal Canadian Engineers 1944 -1945* (2006)
3) *The Wrong Side of the River: The Polish Engineer Company at Arnhem* (2007)
4) *Storm Boat Kings: The 23rd RCE at Arnhem 1944* (1st Ed: 2009)
5) *It Happened Here* (2009)
6) *Basic Function* (2010)
7) *Engineers at the Bridge* (2010)
8) *Encyclopedia of the R.C.E. in WWII Part I: The Field Units* (2010)
9) *Non-Bailey Bridging in Canadian Service* (2010)
10) *War History 11th Field Company, Royal Canadian Engineers 1945* (2011)
11) *A Long Tradition* (2011)
12) *Assault Boats on the Waal* (2011)
13) *Bridging Hell's Highway* (2011)
14) *A Token Force* (2012)
15) *The Bailey Bridge in Canadian Service* (2012)
16) *Allied Attack Boats* (2013)
17) *Commander Royal Engineers* (2013)
18) *Nowhere to Run* (2013)
19) *The Code of History* (2013)
20) *Is There a Straight Road in Scotland?* (2013)
21) *Boats at Arnhem and Other Stories* (2014)
22) *River Assault* (2014)
23) *The Way North* (2014)
24) *Encyclopedia of the R.C.E. in WWII Part II: Lines of Communication Troops* (2014)
25) *War Establishments of the R.C.E, in WWII* (2015)
26) *Bridging the Club Route* (2015)
27) *Two Stories of Storm Boats* (2015)
28) *Pegasus II: The Storm Boat Kings' Perspective* (2015)
29) *Urban Snapshots* (2016)
30) *The Arnhem Conspiracy* (2016)
31) *Paradise Found and Lost* (2016)
32) *Allied Assault Rafts* (2017)
33) *A Bridge on a Bridge* (2017)
34) *Vending Machine Drunk* (2018)
35) *The Long Road Back to Arnhem* (2019)
36) *Time in the Infinite Hallway* (2019)
37) *Special Bridging Force* (2021)
38) *The Hypnotic Hand* with Patricia Bandurka (2021)
39) *The Earthmover in Canadian Service* (2021)

www.ingramcontent.com/pod-product-compliance
Lightning Source LLC
Chambersburg PA
CBHW071750120626
46550CB00002B/733